DAVID STENT is currently Head of Religious Studies at Cams Hill School, Fareham, Hants, where he is also responsible for Community Service links. Formerly Head of Religious Studies at Shirley Warren School, Southampton, he has taught in both state and independent schools and has also lectured for the WEA. He is the author of *Religious Studies Made Simple,* published by Heinemann.

GCE O-Level Passbooks

BIOLOGY, R. J. Whitaker, B.Sc. and
J. M. Kelly, B.Sc., M.I.Biol.

CHEMISTRY, C. W. Lapham, M.Sc.

COMPUTER STUDIES, R. J. Bradley, B.Sc.

ECONOMICS, J. E. Waszek, B.Sc.(Econ)

ENGLISH LANGUAGE, Robert L. Wilson, M.A.

FRENCH, G. Butler, B.A.

GEOGRAPHY, R. Knowles, M.A.

GEOGRAPHY, BRITISH ISLES,
D. A. Bryant, B.A. and R. Knowles, M.A.

GERMAN, A. Nockels, M.A.

HISTORY, POLITICAL AND
CONSTITUTIONAL (1815–1951),
L. James, B.A., M.Litt.

HISTORY, SOCIAL AND ECONOMIC
(1815–1951), M. C. James, B.A.

HUMAN BIOLOGY, S. R. Cantle,
B.Sc., M.Med.Sci.

MODERN MATHEMATICS, A. J. Sly, B.A.

PHYSICS, B. P. Brindle, B.Sc.

TECHNICAL DRAWING, P. J. Barnett,
M.C.C.Ed., Adv.Dip.Ed.

GCE O-Level and CSE
Passbook

Religious Studies

D. Stent B.Ed.

Published by Charles Letts and Co Ltd
London, Edinburgh and New York

Published 1984 by Charles Letts & Co Ltd
Diary House, Borough Road, London SE1 1DW

1st edition 1st impression
© Charles Letts & Co Ltd 1984
Made and printed by Charles Letts (Scotland) Ltd
ISBN 0 85097 606 5

Contents

Introduction

This book has been prepared with the express needs of CSE and O-Level candidates in mind. For this reason, attention is given to those areas of Religious Studies that feature most in the syllabuses set by the Examining Boards.

Emphasis is placed initially on the Old and New Testaments, as here we find the background to both Jewish and Christian thought. A close study of the New Testament is essential reading for all Examining Boards, whether O-Level or CSE. Sometimes the Gospels are studied as a whole and sometimes separately, but most Examining Boards concentrate on the Synoptic Problem relating to the first three Gospels.

The Bible and current issues is an area assuming greater importance today, as is the study of world religions. These may be investigated from a topical point of view, that is, one which deals with the founders of the religions, the sacred books, or places of pilgrimage. Alternatively, world religions may be studied one by one, so that the student can understand more fully the basic ideas and beliefs of the religion selected for study. Both approaches have their merits and both can be found in examination syllabuses. Where Examining Boards have two parts to the examination, students can study for one paper the more traditional parts of the subject, such as a section from the Old Testament, and, for a separate paper, one of the major world religions.

Today, by common consensus, what was formerly called Scripture, Religious Instruction, Religious Education, and sometimes Divinity, is now generally known as Religious Studies. The reasoning behind this move has been the wish to encourage the study of beliefs and practices in world religions from an objective stance, in the same manner as other examination subjects.

All quotations have been taken from the New English Bible. (New English Bible, © 1970 by permission of Oxford and Cambridge University Presses.)

Part One
The Bible

Chapter 1
Old Testament History to the Division of the Kingdom

The striking fact that emerges from a study of the Old Testament is the Jews' high sense of involvement with God. Although in one light it is an historical account of the Jewish people, in another it is a story of a God-man relationship in which the Jews were chosen as God's people and were separated from other nations by their religion and customs.

At the beginning of the Old Testament it is strongly implied that the God of the people of Israel has always been at the centre of creation and is responsible for it. The book of Genesis states that God made the world and all living things in six days. It is said that he rested on the seventh day which is thus rendered a day of rest called the sabbath. The early mythological stories in Genesis show how he provided everything for man, only to be confronted with man's disobedience of his commands. This is illustrated by the story of Adam and Eve in the Garden of Eden (Genesis 3:1–24), and the account of how Cain killed his brother Abel (Genesis 4:1–16). It is thought that this latter story explains the conflict between the early farming community and the early shepherds.

We are told that, eventually, people became so sunk in wickedness that God regretted having created man. The flood is a symbol of God's judgment, and its message is that he cannot condone sin. Though deserving to be destroyed, mankind was saved from extinction because of Noah 'a righteous man, the one righteous man of his time' (Genesis 6:9). After the flood, God made a covenant with Noah as a representative of the human race. Like all the covenants in the Bible it is an expression of the love and mercy of God despite the frailty of man. The rainbow in the sky is a token of this covenant that God made with man that 'never again shall all living creatures be destroyed by the waters of the flood . . .' (Genesis 9:11).

For the history and religion of the Jewish people, the first personality of real importance was Abraham, the patriarch, or early tribal leader. While we cannot be sure of the historical validity of the events recorded in Genesis as a whole, the narrative as from Genesis 11, which tells us about Abraham, is generally believed to be based on fairly reliable early traditions.

The beginning of the Hebrew religion (Genesis 11:27–12:9)

The book of Genesis explains how a man called Terah moved from Ur in Mesopotamia with his family and travelled to Haran, five hundred miles north. Around 1700 BC, or possibly earlier, Terah's son, Abram, was living in Haran when he received a direct call from God. He was instructed to go to a land that God would show him. There he and his people would be made into a great nation. The fact that he obeyed this call is taken as an example of his faith in God.

Abram took Sarah, his wife, his family and Lot his nephew, to the land of Canaan, which lay between the Mediterranean Sea and the Arabian desert. There they became known as the 'Hebrews', meaning 'those who crossed the river'. Apart from a short stay in Egypt, where he went in search of food, Abram remained in Canaan for the rest of his life. He settled at Hebron, where he built an altar to God (Genesis 13:18). Lot, meanwhile, decided to move to the Jordan valley, where later the wicked cities of Sodom and Gomorrah were destroyed by volcanic fire and brimstone.

The agreement with God (Genesis 15:1–21; 17:1–14)

The covenant with Noah was between God and all mankind but the covenant with Abram was between God and his chosen people–Abram and his descendants. God appeared to him in a vision and announced that his name was to be no longer Abram but Abraham. He revealed to him that he would make a covenant with him and his descendants to be their God forever.

Abraham was promised by God that **he would inherit the land of Canaan** and that **his descendants would be as many as the stars in the sky**. All male members of his family would be charged with the duty of keeping their part of the agreement, or covenant, by the act of **circumcision. God, for his part, would care for and protect them.**

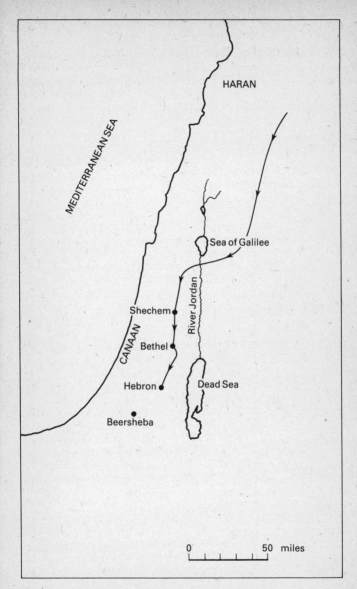

Figure 1. Abraham's journey

The symbolism of the ritual sealing the covenant is very profound and its meaning lies in the idea that the life of an animal is in its blood. The sacrificial victim was regarded as a link between God and man. The bodies of the sacrificed animals were cut in two and normally both parties to the covenant passed between the pieces, so that the two parties were bound together by the life of the animal. In this case, however, only God passed between them as the parties to the covenant were not equal. The smoking brazier and flaming torch are typical pieces of biblical imagery as fire symbolizes the presence of God.

God's promise was to Abraham and his descendants and obviously could not be fulfilled unless Abraham had a child. Some time later, God announced to Abraham that his wife, Sarah, would give birth to a son, but as they were both of a great age, this message caused them much amusement. Abraham already had a son called Ishmael by Hagar, Sarah's Egyptian handmaiden. Ishmael and Hagar were both sent away after the birth of Abraham and Sarah's son, to whom they gave the name Isaac (Genesis 21:8–21).

God tests Abraham's faith and obedience (Genesis 22:1–19)

Abraham had to discover the requirements of his new God. Would he demand human sacrifices in accordance with the custom of the time? Genesis records how Abraham was told by God to take Isaac to a mountain and prepare to sacrifice him to the Lord. It was then that he suddenly saw a ram caught in a thicket and realized that God was providing the ram as an offering in place of his son. Through this, he came to understand that God did not expect human sacrifices from those who worshipped him, but expected faith and obedience. Abraham was to demonstrate not only these qualities but compassion too, as we find in the account of his intercession for the people of Sodom.

When Isaac was older, Abraham sent one of his servants to Haran to find a wife for him from among his own people, as he did not want Isaac to marry a Canaanite woman (Genesis 24:1–67). This servant met by a well a woman called Rebecca who was related to Isaac. She agreed to marry him and returned with the servant to

12

Canaan. Isaac married her and they had twin sons, Esau and Jacob.

Esau and Jacob

Esau, known as the 'hairy' one who enjoyed hunting and later became the father of the Edomites, was the elder of the twins and hence was entitled to the inheritance from his father as his birthright. One day, when he was returning home hungry, he was tricked out of his birthright by his brother, Jacob, who forced him to exchange it for a bowl of soup (Genesis 25:27–34). Whilst Jacob's behaviour is undoubtedly despicable, the point the Bible is making is that Esau thought so little of his birthright (which included the promise made by God to Abraham) that he was prepared to sell it for a trifle. Such a man was obviously unfit to inherit the promise. Later, when Isaac believed himself to be dying, Jacob with the aid of his mother, disguised himself as Esau and tricked his father into giving him his blessing (Genesis 27:1–45). It is plain from the wording of the blessing that material property was being bestowed, rather than spiritual gifts. It is also clear that the blessing was being endorsed by God and that, once given, it could not be withdrawn. Afterwards, Jacob fled north, heading for his uncle Laban's house at Haran.

Jacob's dream

One night on the way to Haran, using a stone for a pillow, Jacob dreamt he saw **a ladder reaching up to heaven with angels ascending and descending**. God appeared to Jacob in his dream and renewed the covenant with him. He promised that Jacob would inherit the land and that he would protect him. It was usual at that time to believe that God communicated to people by the medium of dreams. Jacob assumed that the stone marked a place where God dwelt. For this reason he set up the stone as a sacred pillar and poured oil over it. He called the place 'Bethel', which means 'the house of God'.

When he arrived in Haran, Jacob agreed to work for his uncle Laban for seven years without wages in return for the right to marry his daughter, Rachel. After the seven years, however,

13

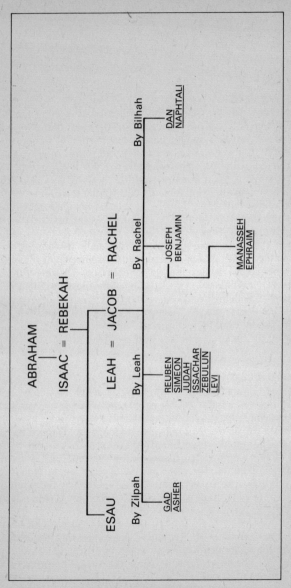

Figure 2. Family tree of the patriarchs

Laban substituted his elder daughter, Leah, and although Jacob did eventually marry Rachel, he had to work for Laban for another seven years. Genesis tells us that he had twelve sons (Genesis 35:23–26). By Leah he had Reuben, Judah, Simeon, Issachar, Levi and Zebulun. By Rachel he had Joseph and Benjamin. By Bilhah, Rachel's handmaid, he had Dan and Naphthali and by Zilpah, Leah's handmaid, he had Gad and Asher.

Eventually, Jacob left Laban and set off with his wives and children to return to Canaan. When he arrived, he heard that Esau was on his way to meet him, accompanied by a large group of people–a prospect which filled him with alarm. In his prayer, he confessed his unworthiness and recalled God's promise to protect him. We learn that Jacob spent that night wrestling with a stranger–a picture of the spiritual struggle of a man tormented by guilt. Jacob wrestled all night and because the man could not throw him, he struck him 'in the hollow of his thigh', dislocating the hip, but still Jacob would not let go until he had received a blessing. The man asked Jacob his name and, when he answered, told him that he would no longer be called 'Jacob' but 'Israel', which means 'soldier of God', because he had striven with God and with men and had prevailed (Genesis 32:27–28). Jacob called the place 'Peniel' because, he said, 'I have seen God face to face and my life is spared.'

Joseph and his brothers–His early years

Joseph was Jacob's favourite son as he was the first-born of Jacob's favourite wife, Rachel. This was the cause of much jealousy among the brothers. His father gave him a coat of many colours, which probably meant that he had chosen him as his heir. He was known to his brothers as a dreamer and related one dream that greatly angered them. He said that, in the dream, he saw their sheaves bowing down to his, suggesting that he would be lord over them. Their jealousy increased to such an extent that they took their brother and put him in a pit. They later sold him to some travelling Ishmaelites (another account describes them as Midianites). These Arab traders took Joseph down to Egypt with them, where he was sold as a slave to Potiphar, one of Pharaoh's

15

officers. Meanwhile, the brothers lied to their father, saying that Joseph had been killed by a wild beast. At this news Jacob was left distraught.

In Egypt Joseph worked well for Potiphar but was falsely accused by Potiphar's wife of assault and subsequently imprisoned. The recording of this episode may indicate the influence of a similar Egyptian story. We read that, while in prison, Joseph **gained a reputation for interpreting dreams**, claiming that he did so with help from God. He explained the chief butler's dream and told him that he would be restored to his post. He also explained the unfortunate chief baker's dream, foretelling he would be hanged! Later events demonstrated that both dreams were interpreted correctly (Genesis 40).

Joseph in power

Two years later Pharaoh had a dream (Genesis 41), and sought its meaning. It was then that the chief butler remembered Joseph and told Pharaoh about his gift for interpreting dreams. Joseph was called out of prison to hear from Pharaoh about his dream. **Joseph predicted that there would be seven years of good crops in Egypt and then seven years of famine**. As a reward for explaining the dream, he was placed in a position of some authority and given responsibility for the storing of grain in granaries.

Pharaoh's dreams were fulfilled in the way that Joseph had predicted, and we read in Genesis 42 of Joseph's brothers 'going down to Egypt from Canaan in search of corn' during the famine, unaware that Joseph had gained a position of such importance. When they met him, they did not even recognize him. Deciding to trick them, he accused them of being spies, and said that they must return with Benjamin, the youngest brother. On their return with their brother they were welcomed with a banquet. Joseph later arranged for a goblet to be placed in Benjamin's sack, and then accused his brothers of theft. It was only after this incident that he revealed his true identity to his brothers and forgave them. Together with their father Jacob, they were provided with a home in Goshen, a fertile region north-east of the Nile delta, in Egypt, where they lived for many years. The story of Joseph as presented in the book of Genesis is particularly colourful. It was quite possibly embellished before it appeared in its current form.

The birth of Moses

The book of Exodus refers to the rise of a Pharaoh who had little sympathy for the Hebrew people and made them slaves. Alarmed by their rapidly-growing numbers, he ordered that all male Hebrew babies should be killed. Popular tradition says that, at this time, a Hebrew mother, to save the life of her baby, placed him in a basket covered with pitch and hid it among the rushes in the River Nile, where he was found by an Egyptian princess. It is difficult to be at all precise about the date of the birth of this boy, called Moses, but the Pharaoh referred to may have been Rameses II, 1290–1224 BC, who used the Hebrews in his massive building programme. Though Moses was brought up in the royal palace, he never ceased to be aware of his Hebrew origin.

Moses' flight (Exodus 2)

Years later, Moses became incensed at the cruelty of the Egyptians to his people and was provoked to kill an Egyptian taskmaster. As a result, he had to flee to the land of Midian at the southern end of the Sinai Peninsula. There he married Zipporah, daughter of a priest called Jethro, who is also recorded as being called Reuel.

The call of Moses (Exodus 3–4)

On one occasion when Moses was at Mount Horeb, looking after his father-in-law's sheep, 'the angel of the Lord appeared to him in the flame of a burning bush' (Exodus 3:2). It is not unusual in the Old Testament to find God associated with trees in this way, just as we saw that God was said to reside in the stone on which Jacob slept. Whatever interpretation of the incident is adopted, it is clear that Moses was greatly aware of the presence of God. He was told that he was standing on holy ground set apart for God, and that the God of his forefathers was speaking to him. **Moses was instructed to tell his people that God had sent him to deliver them from oppression** and when he protested that he was 'slow and hesitant of speech', it was decided that Aaron, his brother, would be his spokesman.

In this incident, God was revealed to Moses as **a God of action**, who would undertake a decisive role in the life of his people but would make special demands of them. **They were to be a holy people, as their God was a holy God**. He was not, therefore, simply a name. The word 'Yahweh' was often used to refer to God and Moses' conception of God may well have been influenced by the religious ideas of the Midianites when he stayed with Jethro, his father-in-law. It is thought that he may also have been influenced by the monotheism (worship of one God) of Akhnaton, Pharaoh Amenhotep IV of Egypt, but this is uncertain.

Pharaoh's disobedience

After the 'meeting' that Moses had with God he left Jethro and returned with his family to Egypt. He approached the Pharaoh there and asked if his people could be allowed to leave Egypt. When Pharaoh refused his request, Moses was assured by God that he would help the people escape from their oppression (Exodus 6:6–8).

Every time Pharaoh relented and agreed to let the people go he subsequently changed his mind. The Egyptians were beset with a series of plagues, which were represented as 'signs and wonders of God' (Exodus 7:14–11:10). We are told that there were ten plagues in all:
  1. The plague of water which changed into blood
  2. The plague of frogs
  3. The plague of maggots
  4. The plague of flies
  5. The plague on the cattle
  6. The plague of boils
  7. The plague of hail
  8. The plague of locusts
  9. The plague of darkness
  10. The plague of the death of the Egyptian first-born.

Before the last plague, the Hebrew people were told to **smear the**

blood of a lamb on their front doors as a sign to the angel who would 'pass over' their houses. They were also instructed to inaugurate a festival, called the **'Passover'** to mark the event. This was probably a development of an already existing religious festival. Some of the plagues may have been related to natural disasters which sometimes occur in Egypt, but tradition has magnified their extent, even claiming that the Hebrews in Goshen were not affected.

The escape from Egypt (Exodus 12:37–15:21)

It is not possible to say exactly how many Hebrews left Egypt but this assorted group of people were convinced that they were being led by God. In contrast to the importance attached to the event by Jews throughout their history, Egyptian records do not mention the occasion at all. The total number involved is therefore unlikely to have been very large. Pursued by the Egyptians, Moses and his people were faced with what seemed to them an impassable sea. Then, at the very moment that the Egyptians were approaching, a strong easterly wind divided the waters, enabling the Hebrews to cross. Perhaps an earth tremor assisted them in their passage over what was probably an extension of the Gulf of Suez, rather than the Red Sea. The Egyptian soldiers following in their heavy chariots were drowned. The book of Exodus represents the events as the work of the God of the Hebrews; the deliverance from Egypt was seen as part of his great plan for the people, and is central in Jewish religion today.

Exodus 15 records the 'Song of Moses' after the Hebrews' escape from the Egyptians: 'I will sing to the Lord, for he has risen up in triumph; the horse and his rider he has hurled into the sea. The Lord is my refuge and my defence, he has shown himself my deliverer.'

Not long after the crossing and during their sojourn in the Wilderness, the people complained to Moses about their conditions, saying that they had been better off in slavery in Egypt! They were now free but without food. They found **quails** which are low-flying birds and ate them (Exodus 16:12–13), and also ate **manna** for bread. This is a sweet substance formed from the

19

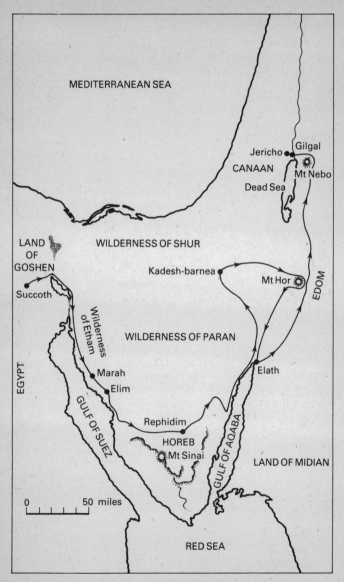

Figure 3. Route taken by the Israelites from Egypt to Canaan

secretions of insects on tamarisk trees, which is boiled before eating (Exodus 16:14–16). On one occasion water was found springing from a rock (Exodus 17:1–7). Once again, these events are represented as acts of God supporting the people in troubled times.

Jethro visits Moses

The visit that Jethro, Moses' father-in-law, made to Moses at this point is quite significant. It is clear that Moses looked up to Jethro for advice and that Jethro acted as a kind of father-figure to him. No doubt Moses learnt a great deal from him and acted on his advice. It has been suggested that Moses adopted the judicial system of the Midianites as a result of his friendship with Jethro. Of this, however, we cannot be certain. What is evident is that he **took Jethro's advice about setting up 'courts of law'**. Jethro was concerned that Moses would wear himself out by dealing with every case himself and so suggested that he delegated some of his authority to others. He told Moses to instruct the people in the law but also to seek out worthy men who could act on his behalf and advise the people. Moses took up the suggestion and dealt only with the more serious cases himself. This was the beginning of permanent courts of law among the people and the origin of the Jewish Council called the Sanhedrin, which became so powerful later in the time of Jesus.

Moses as the law-giver

Moses became his people's law-giver and instructed them in the laws of God as revealed to him at Mount Sinai in the form of the **Ten Commandments**. The exact location of Mount Sinai is not known. The Commandments are also called the '**Decalogue**' and can be found in Deuteronomy 5:6–21 and Exodus 20:2–17. It is useful to note that 1–4 are about God and worship, 5–9 are about conduct in society and 10 is, in a sense, a summary, governing not only conduct but attitudes.

'I am the Lord your God who brought you out of Egypt, out of the land of slavery.'
1. You shall have no other god to set against me.

2. You shall not make or worship idols.
3. You shall not make wrong use of the name of the Lord your God.
4. Keep the Sabbath day holy.
5. Honour your father and your mother.
6. You shall not commit murder.
7. You shall not commit adultery.
8. You shall not steal.
9. You shall not give false evidence against your neighbour.
10. You shall not covet.

The **covenant** that God had made with Abraham was renewed with Moses and the people of Israel, or the Israelites, as they became known. **If they would obey his laws, he would be their God**. Moses built an altar to God with twelve pillars to represent the twelve tribes of Israel. From this date the Israelites were moulded into a community, God's chosen people. They were to have no other gods before him. This is especially emphasized because God had done so much for them:

> Then we cried to the Lord the God of our fathers for help, and he listened to us and saw our humiliation, our hardship and distress; and so the Lord brought us out of Egypt with a strong hand and outstretched arm, with terrifying deeds, and with signs and portents. He brought us to this place and gave us this land, a land flowing with milk and honey.
>
> (Deuteronomy 26:7–9)

At this stage in the history of the people's religion there is no suggestion that there were not other gods apart from Yahweh, but he was the only one they were to worship. They were to do this especially on his day, the sabbath. One day when Moses returned from communing with God, he was angry to discover that the people had attempted to represent God by an image in the shape of a golden calf (Exodus 32), thus breaking the second Commandment. The books of Leviticus, Numbers and Deuteronomy, elaborate on the 'laws' of Moses. These are summed up in the words of the **'Shema'**, meaning 'hear', taken from the first word of Deuteronomy 6:4–5: 'Hear O Israel, the Lord is our God, One Lord, and you must love the Lord your God with all your heart and soul and strength.'

The Israelites made an Ark, or chest known as the **Ark of the Covenant** (Exodus 25:10–22), using acacia wood, to house the tablets on which the Ten Commandments were written, and this was kept in a tent, or **'tabernacle'**. The Levites, who came from Moses' own tribe, looked after the tabernacle. It was believed that the Ark represented the presence of God. Throughout his days with the people in the country south of Beersheba, Moses encouraged them to regard themselves as the people of God. According to the record of these times, the Hebrews spent forty years in the wilderness, though again we cannot be sure about the length of this period.

Joshua as leader of the people

It is likely that the conquest of Canaan was gradual and piecemeal, as suggested in the book of the Judges, rather than a once-for-all event as implied in the book of Joshua. The Israelites conquered the land tribe by tribe over a number of years. They were fighting for religious and political independence.

God promised Joshua, who had been appointed by Moses to succeed him as leader of the Israelites, that he would protect him and help him to conquer the land of Canaan. A new covenant was made with Joshua and the people and, as with Moses, they were to worship God and to obey his laws. One of Joshua's first acts was to send two spies to the city of **Jericho**, which he needed to capture in order to gain control of central Palestine. They were assisted by a woman called Rahab, who helped them escape from the city. The collapse of the walls of the city (Joshua 6:20), may have been due to an earthquake. Because this was Joshua's first conquest, he 'devoted' it to God; all of the inhabitants were killed and the city destroyed. This was in accordance with what was called the **'Cherem'** (ban). The enemies of a particular tribe were considered also to be the enemies of the tribe's god. A battle was fought on behalf of the god and then the spoils of the battle were 'devoted' (given) to him.

After the battle of Jericho, Joshua and his men conquered the town of **Ai**, which was fourteen miles from Jerusalem. It was at Ai that Achan kept some of the spoil which was to be given to God. It is suggested that it was because of Achan's action that they failed in their first attack on the city. Some people think, however, that Bethel may be meant here rather than Ai. A further spectacular victory took place at **Hazor** (Joshua 11), which was nine miles north of the site of Capernaum. With such a series of victories, Joshua led the people in the conquest of the land of Canaan until his death, which is recorded in Joshua 24.

The later chapters of the book of Joshua record how the land of Canaan, a country smaller than Wales, eventually became divided among the tribes of Israel and how they formed themselves into a confederacy of tribes. It should be noted that, as they advanced and then settled in a new region, they took over Canaanite shrines and converted them into shrines for the worship of Yahweh.

The period of the Judges (1200–1025 BC)

The Judges were local heroes or deliverers in the sense that they 'delivered' the people after attacks made by neighbouring tribes and remained in power afterwards to administer justice over a part of the land.

They were charismatic leaders, that is to say they were filled with a spiritual power, and led the Israelites when they tried to conquer further territory. Each of the judges felt convinced that he was called by God and was fighting on his behalf. Often they would claim that the people's misfortunes were caused by their unfaithfulness to God in worshipping other gods and following such practices as ritual prostitution. Indeed, the Judges were prominent at a time when 'every man did what was right in his own eyes' (Judges 17:6). The book of Judges emphasizes that their sins would bring punishment upon the people as a whole. Similarly, if the Israelites placed their trust in God, he would deliver them.

Most of the Judges were associated with places which had their own religious sanctuaries. There may have been more than one Judge 'ruling' over the people in different parts of the land at any one time. In any event, we cannot be sure of the chronological sequence of events in the book of Judges. The most important of the Judges were:

1. **Othniel**, who was called a Kenizzite (that is, a member of an Edomite clan (Judges 3:9–11)) fought against the king of Mesopotamia, or possibly Edom.

2. **Ehud**, the Benjamite, fought and defended the people against King Eglon of Moab (Judges 3:12–30).

3. The prophetess **Deborah** and the warrior leader **Barak**, of the tribe of Naphtali, fought Sisera, leader of the Canaanites, in the Plain of Esdraelon. After the battle Sisera was killed by a woman called Jael with a tent peg. The book of Judges gives an account of the battle in prose and also in verse. The latter is known as 'The Song of Deborah' (Judges 5). It is emphasized in the 'Song' that the God of the Israelites is a jealous God who does not tolerate any competition from other gods.

4. **Gideon** (Judges 6:11–8:35), belonged to the tribe of Manasseh, and was opposed to the worship of other gods. He destroyed the shrine of his father, himself a Baal worshipper. Once again we read of a sacred tree or pole used for purposes of worship. Gideon built a new altar to Yahweh, which his father readily accepted. Gideon also fought against the Midianites and the Amelekites and gained great acclaim from the people, though he refused the title of king.

5. **Jephthah** (Judges 11:1–12:7), freed the people of Gilead from the Moabites, but we also read of Jephthah fighting the Ammonites, as two accounts of the event have been joined together. Jephthah is remembered in particular for the **vow** that he made to sacrifice to God the first person who came out of his house to meet him on his return from battle. To his horror it happened to be his own daughter. We cannot be certain whether he did in fact offer his daughter but the account does illustrate that human sacrifices were still sometimes made by the Israelites.

6. **Samson** This popular hero was a member of the tribe of Dan (Judges 13–16), and fought the Philistines, an invading sea people, who probably came from the Aegean Islands. He was a Nazarite (Numbers 6:1–8), and so did not drink wine or cut his hair. In the story of Samson and his wife, Delilah who deceived him and betrayed him to the Philistines, his strength really lay in his vow not to cut his hair.

The call and work of Samuel

We read about the work of Samuel in the first book of that name. Hannah, wife of Elkanah, lived at Ramah, nine miles from Jerusalem, in about 1025 BC. She longed for a son, whom she vowed she would give to the Lord. Hannah eventually gave birth to a son whom she called Samuel, and to keep her vow she took him as a young boy to Eli, a priest, who guarded the Ark of the Covenant at Shiloh (1 Samuel 1:21–28). Samuel later became a Nazarite (one who dedicates himself to God and takes a vow not to cut his hair or beard or drink wine). It was at Shiloh that **Samuel heard the voice of God**, (which he first mistook for Eli's voice) summoning him to his service (1 Samuel 3:1–21).

> So the child Samuel was in the Lord's service under his master Eli. Now in those days the word of the Lord was seldom heard, and no vision was granted. But one night Eli, whose eyes were dim and his sight failing, was lying down in his usual place, while Samuel slept in the temple of the Lord where the Ark of God was. Before the lamp of God had gone out, the Lord called him, and Samuel answered, 'Here I am,' and ran to Eli saying, 'You called me: here I am.' 'No, I did not call you,' said Eli; 'lie down again.' So he went and lay down. The Lord called Samuel again, and he got up and went to Eli. 'Here I am,' he said; 'surely you called me.' 'I did not call, my son,' he answered; 'lie down again.' Now Samuel had not yet come to know the Lord, and the word had not been disclosed to him. When the Lord called him for the third time, he again went to Eli and said, 'Here I am; you did call me.' Then Eli understood that it was the Lord calling the child; he told Samuel to go and lie down and said, 'If he calls again, say, "Speak Lord; thy servant hears thee." '

It was the beginning of a long and devoted service to Yahweh, his God. Samuel became a Judge of a certain area or circuit and established a base at Ramah.

Eli had two sons, Hophni and Phinehas, who abused their rôle as priests and stole from the offerings the people brought for the Lord. They thought they could overcome the Philistines if they took the Ark of the Covenant with them into battle.

Unfortunately, the plan misfired. The Israelites were defeated, the Ark was captured and both Hophni and Phinehas were killed, as well as many other Hebrews. When Eli heard the news he fell backwards from shock and died of a broken neck. Possession of the Ark brought so much misfortune to the Philistines, however, that they ultimately returned it, though nothing was heard of it after this until the time of David (2 Samuel 6). Samuel stands out in the history of Israel as a great leader of the people and as a prophet speaking on God's behalf. Above all, he was a man the people felt they could trust.

The beginning of the monarchy

While the Judges had ruled over the people on a rather local level, none of them, apart possibly from Abimelech, Gideon's son, had been appointed or had adopted the title of 'king'. Gideon himself had rejected the idea of being a priest-king. It was in the time of Samuel that the people first demanded a king, so as to be in line with the neighbouring countries (1 Samuel 8:1–22).

At this time, there was a considerable amount of contact with neighbouring tribes and this had resulted in the inevitable intermarriage of the people with those whose religion was, as far as the Israelites were concerned, less pure. It was a gradual, almost imperceptible process and one that brought about other influences in its train. It was natural that the people should want to trade with their neighbours but this led to their religion becoming tainted. Canaanite religious influences became merged with the worship of Yahweh.

The desire for a king was, again, seen as natural by many of the people, though not by Samuel. He thought this would mean a lowering of their religious standards because they should obey only God and not a humanly-appointed king. For this reason he was against the move towards a monarchy. The position is not that clear, however, as we shall see.

We are told (1 Samuel 9:1–10:16), that Saul, a member of the Benjamite tribe, was anointed by Samuel at Ramah, and also that Saul was declared king after his victory over the Ammonites

(1 Samuel 11:1–15). In yet another version we read that Samuel was against having a king as he thought this conflicted with the duty of the people to give their first loyalty to God. Samuel was told by God to collect the people together at Mizpah and appoint a king over them. We thus find that the compilers of the Old Testament books sometimes purposely preserved alternative accounts of the same event and set them down side by side, or wove them together. These accounts show how different groups had different opinions about the value of a king.

The reign of Saul (1 Samuel 13–15)

As the first of the Israelite kings, Saul reigned from approximately 1020 BC, for some twenty years, though his reign was not entirely successful and, for him, certainly not a happy one. He probably established a capital at Gibeah. He fought a number of battles against the Philistines and also the Amalekites. **It was after a victory over the Amalekites in a 'holy' war that Saul displeased Samuel**. The defeated Amalekites were to be 'devoted', or given, to Yahweh, just as the people of Jericho were in the time of Joshua, but Saul allowed their king to go free with the best of the spoil. Samuel saw in this act of leniency that Saul would not be the kind of king that he had expected – that is, one who would act as God commanded on all occasions. **Samuel told Saul that God had rejected him as king** (1 Samuel 15:10–35), and after this meeting he never saw Saul again. This rejection was the cause of much of Saul's later depression.

David, son of Jesse, a shepherd boy who was a clever harpist, was called upon to relieve Saul's sadness by his music. Later he became Saul's armour-bearer, the great friend of Jonathan, Saul's son, and married Michal, Saul's daughter. This friendship with Jonathan, together with David's substantial military successes, caused Saul to be jealous of him and it was because of this jealousy and the attempts which Saul made on his life that David was virtually driven into outlawry. David, on the contrary, spared Saul on more than one occasion when he had an opportunity to kill him. For a short while David even joined the Philistines. The news of the death of Saul and Jonathan on Mount Gilboa while fighting the Philistines, caused great sadness to David, as his famous lament demonstrates:

O prince of Israel, laid low in death!
How are the men of war fallen! . . .
Delightful and dearly loved were Saul
and Jonathan;
in life, in death, they were not parted.
They were swifter than eagles,
stronger than lions.
Weep for Saul, O daughters of Israel!
who clothed you in scarlet and rich embroideries,
who spangled your dress with jewels of gold.

(2 Samuel 1:19, 23–24)

The reign of David 1000–960 BC

As with Saul, there are varying accounts of the appointment of
David as king. In one (1 Samuel 16:1–13), he was chosen by
Samuel, and in the other (1 Samuel 17), he was appointed as a
result of a battle against the Philistines, the occasion of his
legendary conquest of the huge Philistine champion, Goliath.
First, David was made king of Judah (2 Samuel 2:1–7), at
Hebron, some twenty miles south of Jerusalem, where he
established his headquarters. Seven years later, he was also made
king of Israel (2 Samuel 5:1–5). He captured Jerusalem from the
Jebusites and made his capital there. The Ark of the Covenant
was taken at this stage from Kirjath-jearim to Jerusalem
(2 Samuel 6:1–17), and the city thus became the religious and
political centre of the kingdom

There were some unattractive aspects to David's reign, however.
This is illustrated by the story of how David had Uriah the Hittite
killed in order to marry his wife, Bathsheba, whom he had
seduced. For this act the prophet Nathan fiercely condemned him.
He told David a story about a poor man who had a single pet lamb
which was very dear to him and his family. One day the man's rich
neighbour had guests and instead of killing a sheep from his own
flocks for the feast, he stole and killed the poor man's pet lamb.
David was incensed, and declared that such an action should be
punished by death. At this point, Nathan drew a parallel between
his story and David's treatment of Uriah.

David's reign was successful, not least for his victories against his

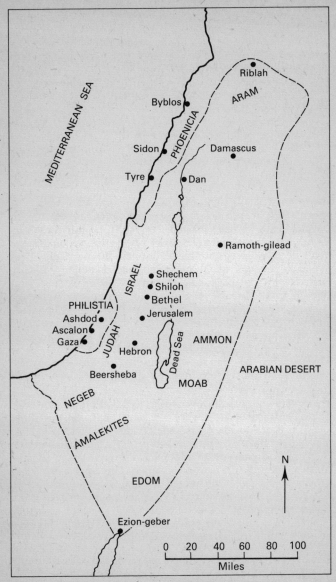

Figure 4. David's empire

neighbours the Philistines, Moabites and Edomites. He built extensively, including a splendid palace for himself and was only prevented from embarking on the building of the Temple by the advice of Nathan. He also initiated trading arrangements with neighbouring countries, including Phoenicia. He organized the people's worship and is the author of at least some of the Psalms which he is said to have written. The Covenant was also renewed with David through Nathan (2 Samuel 7:1–16). David ruled over his people wisely as Yahweh's servant for forty years. He brought the tribes of Israel together, united the kingdom and extended its boundaries.

The reign of Solomon

When Solomon, the son of David by Bathsheba, became king in approximately 960 BC, he requested from God the gift of **wisdom**, and indeed he is said to have written parts of the book of Proverbs (1 Kings 4:29–34). A famous example of his wisdom is shown in his judgment of the dispute of the two women who both claimed to be the mother of a baby (1 Kings 3:16–28).

One of Solomon's first ventures was to build a magnificent **Temple** to God (1 Kings 5). Assisted by Hiram, king of Tyre, who provided many building materials, he took seven years to complete it. Since the architects were Phoenicians, it is not surprising to learn that it was styled along Phoenician lines, a point that would not have endeared it to the people of Israel. Solomon then built a **palace** for himself and many other buildings. All of these projects inevitably drained the resources of the country and for this reason Solomon introduced a system of **taxation** whereby the country was divided into administrative areas. Taxes were exacted in kind as well as in money, and Solomon also **conscripted labour**. At one time he was forced to give Hiram twenty towns of his kingdom in order to repay him for his assistance (1 Kings 9:10–11).

Despite the taxation and the enforced labour, however, his reign was a happy one. There was ample food (Kings 4:25), and Solomon attracted the admiration of such people as the Queen of Sheba, the country later known as Ethiopa. In a material sense, many people may have benefited from his reign, but in a religious sense, it could be said that the country did not benefit. Solomon's tolerance towards the religious practices of his many wives, who pursued other gods and built shrines to worship them, was one reason for the break-up of the kingdom on his death in 922 BC.

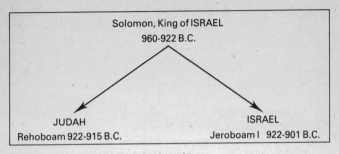

Figure 5. The division of the kingdom

The division of the kingdom on the death of Solomon

On Solomon's death, **Rehoboam**, his son, made no attempt to fulfil the wishes of the people who complained about the taxes and enforced labour. The ten northern tribes rebelled and followed **Jeroboam**, himself a northener, and they formed Ephraim or Israel, which became known as the Northern Kingdom. Jeroboam established an administrative centre at Shechem and later set up the sanctuaries of Bethel and Dan so that the people could worship and sacrifice there instead of going down to Jerusalem. Jeroboam's son, Omri, built and established Samaria as his capital. The tribe of Judah, meanwhile, together with the tribe of Benjamin, formed the Southern Kingdom of Judah, with a capital at Jerusalem.

Chapter 2
The Old Testament Prophets

On many occasions the Old Testament refers to the work of 'prophets', that is, men who became filled with the spirit of God and felt compelled to speak out in his name. They may have been 'ecstatic' prophets, who became emotionally involved in their utterances (examples of these are Elijah and Elisha) or they may have been 'writing' prophets, such as Amos, Hosea, Isaiah and Jeremiah, who have books attributed to them. Such a broad classification cannot always be made and certainly all of the writing prophets were particularly moved by what they saw and heard about their country's ills. Indeed, the prophets are known for their out-spoken comments on and criticisms of the social and religious problems of their day, which they expressed some time before their words were committed to writing.

The ninth-century prophets Elijah and Elisha, together with the 'writing' prophets who followed them, made their pronouncements to the people of Israel on God's behalf, expressing what they felt to be his will. Often they **condemned the injustices and irreligious practices** that they saw and were at odds with the civil and sometimes even the religious authorities, as well as with the people themselves. They spoke to the people of Israel and to the people of Judah, and at times to both countries together.

Elijah

Elijah, a Tishbite from Gilead, whose name means 'my God is Yahweh', first appeared in the northern kingdom in about the year 890 BC, during the reign of King Ahab, (869–850 BC). Elijah seems to have been a highly-strung ascetic figure with immense courage. He denounced the unfaithfulness of the people who had forsaken the worship of Yahweh to follow other gods. Ahab had married Jezebel, daughter of a king of Tyre. A determined woman, she brought into Israel the worship of her own Phoenician gods, along with an attendant retinue of four hundred and fifty priests whom she introduced into the royal court. Her aim in doing this was to abolish the worship of the God of the Israelites altogether.

33

1 Kings 17 tells us that, at this time, there was a long period of drought during which Elijah was fed by ravens and drank from the brook Cherith. When it eventually ran dry, he lodged with a poor widow in Zarephath and throughout his stay, her meagre supply of flour and oil never ran out. This woman's son fell ill and died but was restored to life by Elijah.

After three years, God instructed Elijah to tell King Ahab that the drought would soon come to an end. Elijah realized that it was time for him to **condemn the pagan practices** that he saw around him. He knew that if he said nothing, true worship of Yahweh would soon disappear. This was the beginning of a clash between king and prophet. Though apparently Elijah was of some standing in the local community and was known to the other prophets (2 Kings 2:1–18), he found himself alone in his forthright denouncements of the people's shortcomings. He mocked the gods of the prophets of Baal (1 Kings 18:27), challenging them on Mount Carmel to **a contest as to who could successfully cause a fire to ignite on the respective altars of Baal and Yahweh**. After the complete failure of the prophets of Baal, Elijah, with Yahweh's assistance, succeeded in doing precisely this. He urged the people to return to the worship of Yahweh, the living and personal God, and reject the useless gods who would never aid them. There was a positive reaction from the people in favour of Yahweh, at least temporarily, and the prophets of Baal were all put to death.

In danger of being killed by Jezebel, Elijah fled to Mount Horeb, where he sought refuge, He entered a cave and it was here that he received the word of God–not in the dramatic ways he expected, but in the silence of his receptive heart. He was assured that he was not alone in speaking out on God's behalf, as he had feared in his panic and exhaustion. There would be many witnesses for God ready to defend him. He was told that Elisha was to take his place, and would continue his work.

1 Kings 19:19–21 records the call of Elisha which took place while he was ploughing with twelve pairs of oxen. Elisha was permitted by Elijah to kiss his father and mother goodbye, and from that moment he followed Elijah as his disciple. Such was the call of God. The response was to be immediate.

Elijah attacked the king for his attitude towards the poor, as the story of **Naboth and his vineyard** clearly indicates (1 Kings 21). Naboth had a vineyard in Jezreel which Ahab wished to acquire for himself. Naboth refused to part with it, claiming that it was his family's inheritance. When Jezebel heard of this she had Naboth falsely accused of cursing God and the king, as a result of which he was stoned to death. Ahab was condemned by Elijah for this and was told in no uncertain terms that disaster would befall him and his family. The conversation that took place between the two men is recorded in 1 Kings 21:20–22.

Throughout his prophetic career, Elijah never wavered in his encouragement of the people's worship of Yahweh, which was to be wholehearted and unswerving. It seems fitting, then, to read in 2 Kings 2:1 that he did not die but ascended into heaven in a chariot of fire in a whirlwind. It must be noted, however, that, at this time, the Israelites had no developed belief in a life after death. It was believed that, in some way, God had taken Elijah to be with him. Later, it was thought that Elijah would return to prepare a messianic age.

Elisha

Elisha was appointed by Elijah to succeed him (2 Kings 2:1–15). We are told that the 'spirit of Elijah' fell on him. Elisha is depicted as of a gentler disposition than Elijah. A number of legendary stories is associated with him, such as the purifying of the water supply at Jericho (2 Kings 2:19–22); the miraculous supplying of water to the three kings' army (2 Kings 3:4–20); the filling of a widow's vessels with oil, which gave her money to redeem her sons from slavery (2 Kings 4:1–7); and the bringing back to life of the Shunammite's son (2 Kings 4:31–37).

Perhaps the most famous story connected with Elisha, however, is **the healing of Naaman, the leper**, (2 Kings 5). Naaman was a Syrian general who suffered from leprosy and Elisha was asked to heal him. Elisha commanded Naaman to bathe seven times in the river Jordan, telling him that he would then be cured. At first, Naaman asked why Abana and Pharpar, two rivers of Damascus, would not do just as well but finally he resorted to the river Jordan and after bathing seven times was cured of his disease. From that time onwards, Naaman became a follower of Yahweh.

Elisha played an important part in what became known as the **prophetic revolution**. This was a revival of religious fervour and was so called because it was the prophets who brought about a change of rule in the country so as to ensure that the king and people worshipped Yahweh and did not succumb to the temptation of worshipping foreign gods. Elisha sent a prophet to anoint **Jehu**, an officer in the army at Ramoth Gilead, who would act on God's behalf and purge the country of Baal worship. Jehu undertook this duty with great enthusiasm, killing all those who were members of the house of Ahab, including Jezebel. He then became king himself.

It is interesting to note the similarity between the accounts of Elijah and that of Elisha. This has prompted many scholars to suggest that the two were really one prophet. We have to remember, however, that it is not at all unusual in the Bible–Old Testament and New Testament–to find several accounts of events. Elijah and Elisha both separate the waters of Jordan by hitting them with Elijah's cloak and both bring a child back to life in the same way. Yet they have their individual characteristics and these go to suggest that they were indeed separate prophets working on God's behalf.

Amos

Amos was the first of the writing prophets and also the first of the twelve 'minor' prophets, who were so called because the books attributed to them were shorter in length than the books of the 'major' prophets, Isaiah, Jeremiah and Ezekiel. In other respects, however, it must be said that there is nothing minor about Amos and the prophets who followed him.

Amos began his work about the year 760 BC, in the northern kingdom, during the reign of Jeroboam II (786–746 BC). This period was noted for its prosperity and affluent living. It was this very prosperity that was to cause Amos so much anguish due to its improper use by the people. Like all the prophets with the exception of Hosea, he came from the southern kingdom of Judah. He is thought to have been 'one of the sheep farmers of Tekoa' (Amos 1:1), which was some twelve miles south of Jerusalem. Amos became so distressed at what he heard about the social and religious conditions in the northern kingdom and at Bethel in particular that he travelled there to deliver judgment on the people.

The first messages of Amos were predictions of doom for the people of other countries, such as Syria, Philistia, Phoenicia, Edom, Ammon and Moab. His aim was to demonstrate that **Yahweh was the God of all nations**. He then proceeded to rebuke the people of the northern kingdom for their wrongdoings. The rich were mistreating the poor who had no chance of obtaining justice. He clearly saw himself as **God's spokesman condemning social evils**:

> These are the words of the Lord:
> For crime after crime of Israel
> I will grant them no reprieve,
> because they sell the innocent for silver
> and the destitute for a pair of shoes.
> They grind the heads of the poor into the earth
> and thrust the humble out of their way.
>
> (Amos 2:6–7)

The very idea of such 'class' distinctions seemed, to Amos, to go against the spirit of the original covenant with God. God himself hated such a situation (Amos 6:8). Perhaps they should not be God's people after all. The poor were being given short weight in change, and while children were being accepted as payment for debts, the rich women of the town were grossly over-indulged.

Such happenings enraged Amos because **he saw religion largely in terms of what was right and wrong**. God did not delight in the people's feasts and burnt offerings (Amos 5:21–27), but in justice and fair treatment. It must come as no surprise to us to hear that his messages were not well received. Amaziah, the priest at Bethel, told Amos to get out of the city (Amos 7:10–13), and return to his own country.

Despite such opposition, **Amos continued to rebuke the people and referred to a coming judgment which would befall them because of their**

wickedness. Such judgment would be inescapable (Amos 9:1–4). Justice would 'roll on like a river and righteousness like an ever-flowing stream' (Amos 5:24). Because of such utterances, Amos has often been called the 'Prophet of Doom'. He wanted the people to repent of their wickedness. Then **after the judgment the people would be restored** (Amos 9:8–15). They were still God's people, whom he had chosen (Amos 3:1–2). They had to realize that God is a righteous God and so expects righteousness from his people. They were to practise true religion by seeking good throughout their lives and so abandoning their evil ways.

Amos includes in his book the first reference to the **Day of the Lord** which later became an important concept in Jewish thought. This would be an occasion when God would himself deliver his people, his chosen ones. There would be a golden age at that time. But what sort of occasion would that be? Amos is quite specific:

Fools who long for the day of the Lord,
what will the day of the Lord mean to you?
It will be darkness, not light.
It will be as when a man runs from a lion,
and a bear meets him,
or turns into a house and leans his hand on the wall,
and a snake bites him.
The Day of the Lord is indeed darkness,
not light,
a day of gloom with no dawn.

(Amos 5:18–20)

The book of Amos records for us three of the prophet's visions which form a significant part of his message. In chapter 7:1–3, Amos saw a **plague of locusts** hatching out as the corn is beginning to sprout and interpreted this as a sign that the nation would be destroyed. In chapter 7:7–9 he saw a **plumb-line placed against a wall** to test its uprightness and concluded from this that God was testing the 'uprightness' of Israel and had found it badly out of true. The wall was bound to collapse sooner or later: Israel was not fit to survive. Amos' final vision (Amos 8:1–3) was of **a basket of ripe summer fruit**. The Hebrew word for this reminded him of the word for 'end'–the end of Israel.

Hosea

Amos was succeeded by a man who addressed the people in rather different circumstances. In contrast to the prosperity of the reign of Jeroboam II already mentioned, and the peace and tranquillity that permitted it, Hosea spoke to the people when there was war with Assyria and virtual anarchy in the country.

The prophet Hosea began his work in the northern kingdom where he lived, a little while after Amos. He directed his prophecies to the people of the north and Bethel in particular. He has often been called the **'Prophet of Loving Kindness'**, as he **demonstrated God's great love for the people**, as opposed to the concept of God held by Amos, which was of a God of justice, or righteousness. **Hosea saw a parallel between God's love for the people who had broken their relationship with God, and his own unfortunate marriage**. He had married Gomer, who was unfaithful to him and yet he could not cease to love her. Both priests and people had broken the covenant with God and religious, political and moral decay had set in. In every way they had ceased to be God's people: in politics, in social life and in religion. They had completely forsaken the Lord and given themselves over to immorality and the worship of images.

Hosea's wife may have been a prostitute before he married her and continued to be unfaithful to him. She bore him three children, to whom he gave prophetic names. He called his first son **Jezreel** (Hosea 1:4) – this was the name of the city where Jehu, on the instructions of Elijah, had slaughtered the household of Ahab. Hosea, with his insight into the love of God, condemned such butchery and declared that the descendents of Jehu would be punished because of the bloodshed of Jezreel. Hosea's second child was a daughter, whom he called **Lo-ruhama**, meaning 'no mercy' (Hosea 1:6), for it seemed inconceivable that God could forgive Israel. He named his third child—a son—**Lo-ammi**, which means 'not my people' (Hosea 1:9), for he believed that God would disown Israel. As his understanding of the love and forgiveness of God grew, he abandoned this idea and realized that, if Israel repented, God would forgive and restore the nation.

Despite his wife's continued unfaithfulness to him, Hosea did not stop loving her and paid fifteen pieces of silver, a homer of barley, that is about eleven bushels, and a measure of wine, to buy her back (Hosea 3:2). In the same way, **God would have mercy on Israel and would bring her back to true worship**. He would not give her up but would treat her tenderly. He would welcome the people back after their backsliding. **Repentance** was necessary, first, however, and they could expect **punishment for their unfaithfulness**. After this punishment they should be loyal to Yahweh.

> Return O Israel, to the Lord your God; for you have stumbled in your evil courses. Come with your words ready, come back to the Lord; say to him, "Thou dost not endure iniquity. Accept our plea, and we will pay our vows with cattle from your pens . . ." I will heal their apostasy; of my own bounty will I love them; for my anger is turned away from them.
>
> (Hosea 14:1–2, 4)

The punishment predicted by both Amos and Hosea came with the capture of Samaria by Sargon II, the Assyrian king, who, in 722 BC, deported many of the people to Assyria. This effectively meant the end of the kingdom of Israel. When foreigners were forcibly brought into a country by the Assyrians, to break down the national spirit, they inter-married with the local inhabitants and thus introduced their own ideas and customs from their religions. The writing prophets and the writers of the historical books in the Old Testament suggest that it was the unfaithfulness of the people in their worship of Yahweh that led to the fall of the kingdom of Israel.

Isaiah of Jerusalem

Not very much is known about the prophet Isaiah, who prophesied in Jerusalem in the southern kingdom, a little later than Amos and Hosea, over a period of forty years. Uncertainty must remain about the suggestion made by some scholars that he was an aristocrat. It is believed that Isaiah lived during the reigns of five kings of Judah: Uzziah, in the last year of whose reign (740 BC) he received his call; Jotham, Ahaz, Hezekiah, who was responsible for a number of religious reforms, and Manasseh, in whose reign it is said that Isaiah was sawn asunder. Manasseh was also responsible for the reintroduction of Baal worship and sacred prostitution and even the practice of offering human sacrifices and of consulting the dead.

Isaiah's teachings are preserved in chapters 1–39 of the book 'Isaiah', apart from chapters 24–27 and chapters 34–35, which are thought to come from a later period. The remaining chapters, from 40 to 66, are believed to have been written after his death by another prophet. His call to the prophetic rôle is described in Isaiah 6:1–8. It took place when Isaiah was experiencing a form of trance in the Temple at Jerusalem; he felt that he was in God's heavenly presence and saw a vision of God seated on his throne. An angel touched Isaiah's lips with burning coals from the altar which he interpreted as a sign that God was cleansing him. Isaiah was acutely aware of his own unworthiness before the holiness of God, as the following passage indicates:

> Holy, holy, holy, is the Lord of Hosts:
> the whole earth is full of his glory . . .
> Woe is me! I am lost,
> for I am a man of unclean lips . . .

(Isaiah 6:3, 5)

For Isaiah, the chief characteristic of God was holiness, that is perfect goodness and purity.

Like Amos before him, Isaiah complained that the poor were being oppressed and that there was no justice in the land which was full of corruption. The people had failed completely to lead good and upright lives. He therefore **warned them of the judgment which would surely come to them unless they repented and changed their**

ways. This judgment would come in the shape of the invading Assyrian king (Isaiah 10:5 and 6). Isaiah urged the people not to rebel against the Assyrian forces by joining with Egypt, for the efforts of those who did so would be useless. They were to trust only in Yahweh for he was responsible for all history and it was with him that they shared a special relationship.

A new age would dawn and there would be a **reign of peace and righteousness** under a descendant of the house of David. We find this description of the '**Prince of Peace**' and the conditions in which he will reign:

> The people who walked in darkness
> have seen a great light:
> light has dawned upon them,
> dwellers in a land as dark as death.
> Thou hast increased their joy and given
> them great gladness;
> they rejoice in thy presence as men rejoice
> at harvest,
> or as they are glad when they share out the spoil;
> for thou hast shattered the yoke that burdened them,
> the collar that lay heavy on their shoulders,
> the driver's goad, as on the day of Midian's defeat.
> All the boots of trampling soldiers
> and the garments fouled with blood
> shall become a burning mass,
> fuel for fire.
> For a son has been born for us, a son given to us
> to bear the symbol of dominion on his shoulder;
> and he shall be called
> in purpose wonderful, in battle God-like,
> Father for all time, Prince of peace.
> Great shall the dominion be,
> and boundless the peace
> bestowed on David's throne and on his kingdom,
> to establish it and sustain it
> with justice and righteousness
> from now and for evermore.
> The zeal of the Lord of Hosts shall do this.

(Isaiah 9:2–7)

Neighbouring countries were not immune from the wrath of Isaiah, however, and Babylon, Philistia, Moab, Egypt, and Arabia, were all equally denounced, (Isaiah 13–23). Yet Isaiah also had visions of a brighter future. Some of the people would survive the calamities that would befall the country (Isaiah 10:21), and they were promised a sign, that of a child, who would share the sufferings of the people. Isaiah was **the first prophet to speak of a messiah**, or 'anointed one' (Isaiah 9:2–7 and 11:1–9), who would 'judge the poor with justice and defend the humble in the land with equity' (Isaiah 11:4). Finally, Jerusalem would be the centre of religion. It would be a holy city in a New Age.

Micah

Unlike Isaiah, who, as we have seen, was a city man, the prophet Micah came from a small town called Moresheth-gath, some twenty-five miles south-west of Jerusalem, in the southern kingdom. He was probably a contemporary of Isaiah and his teachings were similar to those of Isaiah and the other writing prophets who had preceded him. **He rebuked the people for their greed and the landowners for their treatment of the poor** (Micah 2:2). Even the priests were failing to carry out their duties properly.

Social injustices were rife and no one could get a fair deal. Corruption was widespread and the country was full of wickedness:

'Loyal men have vanished from the earth, there is not one upright man. All lie in wait to do murder, each man drives his own kinsman like a hunter into the net. They are bent eagerly on wrongdoing, the officer who presents the requests, the judge who gives judgment for reward, and the nobleman who harps on his desires.'

(Micah 7:2–3)

What hope was there in such a situation? Micah continues in the same vein: (verses 5 and 6):

Trust no neighbour, put no confidence in your closest friend; seal your lips even from the wife of your bosom. For son maligns father, daughter rebels against mother,

43

daughter-in-law against mother-in-law, and a man's enemies are his household.

In a country where one person exploits another there is no hope for anyone. So what was Micah's advice for the people?:

God has told you what is good; and what is it that the Lord asks of you? Only to act justly, to love loyalty, to walk wisely before your God.

If they followed his advice and truly sought God's ways then all would be well. God would send the messiah and he would deliver the people. The age of peace would then begin.

The achievements of Josiah

In the eighteenth year of the reign of Josiah, that is in 621 BC, **the 'book of the law' was found in the Temple at Jerusalem** when it was being rebuilt. The book was taken to the king who was greatly shaken by its contents. It is likely that it contained part of the book of Deuteronomy, perhaps chapters 12–26, which consist of addresses to the people by an unknown author or authors, urging them to renew the covenant with Yahweh. The way to do this was to follow a set of laws described in the book of Deuteronomy.

Josiah called the people together and made a special covenant to follow the law. He pledged that the book that they had found would be obeyed in its entirety (2 Kings 23:1–3). The reforms which followed included the establishment of Jerusalem as a focal point of worship. It was thought that in this way there would be less chance of the people being tempted by the worship of other gods. All idols were destroyed and the worship associated with these idols was banned. Everything connected with the worship of foreign gods was thrown out. Mediums who attempted to make contact with the dead were ordered not to practise and astral cultic rituals and human sacrifice which had appeared again, were to be stopped.

Josiah was killed at Megiddo by the forces of Pharaoh Necho II in 609 BC. He was succeeded by his son, Jehoahaz, but after three months Necho despatched him to Egypt and made Eliakim king, whose name was changed to Jehoiakim. The Egyptians were later defeated by the Babylonians at Carchemish in 605 BC.

The role of Jeremiah

The prophet Jeremiah came from a priestly family of Anathoth, four miles from Jerusalem. He was a great spiritual teacher who preached from the time of Josiah, about 626 BC, to the period of the Exile in 586 BC, when the Jews were transported to Babylon after their defeat by the armies of Nebuchadnezzar. His work therefore stretched over a forty-year period. From the account of his call by God (Jeremiah 1:4–19), we receive the picture of a shy and retiring young man who plainly had no wish to be a prophet. He claimed that he was too young but God assured him that he would guide him. He began preaching in the Temple at Jerusalem (Jeremiah 7:1–15), and urged the people to mend their ways, as once again pagan practices were being introduced into the country, such as idolatry, child sacrifices and the worship of idols, besides a wide variety of social evils. All of these were now very familiar to the prophets. So zealous was Jeremiah in his denunciations of the people's immorality and evil ways, that he had to be rescued by the Temple priests and was told by them that further preaching in the Temple would not be possible. For this reason he employed an assistant called Baruch, who acted as his secretary, writing down everything he said. When King Jehoiakim heard the words of Jeremiah read to him he tore up each section of the scroll once it had been read and threw it onto the fire. Jeremiah later rewrote his prophecies and even added more to those he had already written (Jeremiah 36).

Jeremiah prophesied that judgment would come upon the people because of their wickedness. **Unless they changed their ways and stopped worshipping other gods, they would be driven into exile**. God showed Jeremiah that the nation of Israel was to God like clay in the hands of a potter: if it is evil, that is, marred, he will destroy it, but if it is good, that is, sound, he will use it (Jeremiah 18:1–10). **There would have to be an inward and personal response on the part of the people to God's call. What was needed was a new relationship with God. There would be a new covenant which would be written on their hearts** (Jeremiah 31:31–33). Outward, mechanical worship would be of no use at all. Everyone would have to answer for his own sins. There would thus be a new community of people.

Jeremiah was concerned about the position of the individual

person before God. The new covenant would be of a much more personal nature than the covenant that they knew. That had been written on tablets of stone. The people were to experience now the kind of relationship that was founded on personal faith:

> The time is coming, says the Lord, when I will make a new covenant with Israel and Judah. It will not be like the covenant I made with their forefathers when I took them by the hand and led them out of Egypt. Although they broke my covenant I was patient with them, says the Lord. But this is the covenant which I will make with Israel after those days, says the Lord; I will set my law within them and write it on their hearts; I will become their God and they shall become my people. No longer need they teach one another to know the Lord; all of them, high and low alike, shall know me, says the Lord, for I will forgive their wrongdoing and remember their sin no more.

> (Jeremiah 31:31–34)

Like those before him, **Jeremiah urged the people to trust in Yahweh and not to attempt to join any political alliances**. Just as Isaiah encouraged the people not to resist the Assyrians, so Jeremiah urged them not to provoke the Babylonians, who were sure to come. For these unwelcome words the prophet soon found himself imprisoned!

Nebuchadnezzar and the Babylonian army besieged the city in 597 BC, just as Jeremiah had foretold (2 Kings 24:8–17). The king, Jehoiakim, was killed and his son, Jehoiachin, surrendered to the invading forces. He was deported to Babylon, which was some six hundred miles away, and Mattaniah, Jehoiachin's uncle (renamed Zedekiah) succeeded him as king of Judah, until he too rebelled. After witnessing the slaying of his sons before his eyes, Zedekiah was blinded, bound with fetters of brass and carried captive to Babylon, along with some of the people of Judah.

It appears from the book of Jeremiah that there may have been three deportations of Jews from Judah:
1. Jeremiah 52:28 suggests 3023 people were deported to Babylon, probably with Jehoiakim in 597 BC.
2. Jeremiah 52:29 suggests 832 people were deported, probably with Zedekiah in 586 BC.

3. Jeremiah 52:30 refers to a further deportation of 745 people. It is likely therefore that few in comparison with the total population of Jews in Judah were sent into exile. The total of these deportations amounts to only 4600 people. Nevertheless, the future of the religion of Israel and perhaps the future of the nation rested with this exiled minority.

Jeremiah was freed by the Babylonians on their arrival and was allowed to remain in Jerusalem which was now in ruins since the Palace and the Temple and many other buildings had been destroyed. He wrote to the exiles (Jeremiah 29), giving advice on how they were to conduct themselves in Babylon, where they were to remain for a long time. He encouraged them to build houses, prepare gardens, marry and establish homes, and also expect to see their grandchildren. His general advice was that the exiles should make the best they could of the situation.

At this time, Judah was formed into a province, with Gedaliah as governor. On his assassination the province was merged with the northern territory and governed from Samaria. Jeremiah was taken against his will to Egypt at some stage after this by those responsible for the assassination of Gedaliah. He remained there for the rest of his days.

The basic teaching of Jeremiah was similar to that of the other writing prophets: the people had committed acts of wickedness for which they would be punished, yet God was a loving God and he would love and care for his chosen people. **The idea that a person could enter into a personal relationship with God and be personally responsible to him was, however, a new feature in the religious thought of the people and this is Jeremiah's distinctive contribution**. It represented a change of emphasis in Jewish thought that was to be of considerable significance in the years to come.

Chapter 3
The Jewish Exile and Return

The exile to Babylon in Mesopotamia, the land between the rivers Tigris and Euphrates, where the Jews settled by the river Chebar, was by no means the end of the Jewish people as a nation. Their captivity lasted for sixty years (597–537 BC), though it was not a captivity in the usual sense of the word. The people were allowed a fair degree of freedom, as we have already seen from a study of Jeremiah's letter to the exiles. It is also evident from the book of Ezra that they were not confined to one particular area. Despite this freedom and the fact that they were allowed to practise their religion, they found the adjustment to a new life extremely difficult at first. The book of Psalms conveys to us some of their initial thoughts: By the rivers of Babylon we sat down and wept when we remembered Zion . . . How could we sing the Lord's song in a foreign land?' (Psalm 137:4). Then they realized that God was not left behind in Jerusalem since he is, in fact, everywhere (Psalm 139).

The exiles were particularly concerned as to how they would maintain the purity of their faith pending their deliverance, which many hoped would come soon. They were living in a land where strange gods were worshipped and where they had no Temple. They hoped that their former king, Jehoiachin, would lead them back in due course to their own country. Jehoiachin was released from prison in 561 BC, by Evil-merodach, who succeeded Nebuchadnezzar, as ruler of Babylon.

Jeremiah, in his letter to the exiles, was not the only one to tell them to settle down to their new life. The prophet Ezekiel's teachings follow a similar line. **The people began to meet for readings from the scriptures in each other's homes,** including that of Ezekiel. The synagogue as a meeting place may well go back in origin to such house gatherings. The **scriptures were carefully written down** and the various versions of stories, events, and traditions were blended together into a continuous narrative. It became **a great time for study of the Jewish Law** and it was then that the Jewish Law codes were drawn up in the form we now have them in the Old Testament. The religious leaders often met together to draw up rules relating to Temple worship for the time when they would return to Jerusalem. Every means was taken to preserve the identity of the Jewish faith. **A new emphasis was placed on circumcision as demonstrating the Jews' commitment to the covenant with God.** Greater importance was attached to **dietary laws**. However, because they were living far away from their Temple at Jerusalem, their religion had to become less dependent on rites and rituals.

Ezekiel

During the fifth year of the captivity, the priest and prophet Ezekiel, who had been taken into captivity with Jehoiachin in 597 BC, received his call by means of a vision when he was at Tell-Abib, by the river Chebar (Ezekiel 1–3). In Ezekiel's description of the supernatural forms that appeared in his vision, he may have been influenced by the Babylonian images that would have been familiar to him. We are told that, in his vision, he made God's words his own by actually swallowing the scroll on which they were written! **From the visions and trances to which Ezekiel refers, it is clear that God is far above and vastly different from man, although he does have dealings with man**.

Ezekiel was obviously writing at a time when the people of Israel had established themselves in exile since he was living in his own house (Ezekiel 3:24), although he addressed some of his words to those still in Jerusalem. He may, in fact, have returned to Jerusalem for some period as he certainly showed a fair knowledge of events there. **He condemned the wicked ways of the people of Israel before the holiness of God and predicted the second fall of Jerusalem**, which had not by then taken place (Ezekiel 4–5). The people were not to store up false hopes about a speedy return. At first no-one would listen to him. Like Jeremiah, **Ezekiel preached that everyone was responsible for his own actions**.

The righteous man shall reap the fruit of his own righteousness, and the wicked man the fruit of his own wickedness. It may be that a wicked man gives up his sinful ways and keeps all my laws, doing what is just and right. That man shall live; he shall not die. None of the offences he

49

has committed shall be remembered against him; he shall live because of his righteous deeds.

(Ezekiel 18:20–22)

For Ezekiel it was the present attitude of a man that mattered most, especially if he had put aside his evil ways. He made it plain that **the present predicament of the people was the result of the country's sins as a whole**. Furthermore, other countries such as Ammon, Moab, Edom, Philistia, Tyre, Sidon and Egypt, did not escape his condemnation (Ezekiel 25–32).

Ezekiel did hold out hope for the future however, for later **the nation would be restored**. The exiles were compared with old bones or carcases but they would be given new life (Ezekiel 37:1–14). **Ezekiel saw God as the Shepherd of the people, who would find his lost sheep and would return them to their own land** (Ezekiel 34:11–13). The Temple would be restored (Ezekiel 40–48), in the new Jerusalem with a new community, which would be a 'kingdom of priests'. Here we see the priestly rather than the prophetic influence of Ezekiel. He regarded religious observances as particularly important.

Deutero-Isaiah

The prophet whose work is embodied in Isaiah 40–55 is nowadays usually called 'Second' or 'Deutero-' Isaiah, because his name is not known. He was clearly not the same person as Isaiah of Jerusalem, who is responsible for much, but not all, of Isaiah 1–39. There are many indications that Deutero-Isaiah lived much later than (First) Isaiah, and that the background to his ministry was the exile in Babylon, at that time nearing its end. He could thus be called the Isaiah of Babylon to distinguish him from the other 'Isaiahs'. Certainly the references confirm that the writer cannot be the same as the Isaiah of chapters 1–39, as in speaking of a deliverer (Isaiah 45:1–4), he mentions the Persian king Cyrus, who reigned from 550–529 BC, some 150 years after the events recorded in Isaiah 1–39.

The prophet told the people to trust in God who was seen as all-powerful (Isaiah 45:5–7) and pointed out how useless it was to worship an idol which was merely made by man and lifeless. **God who had created all things, had formed Israel to be his servant**, whom he would never forget (Isaiah 44:9 and 21). **The other nations of the world were to be saved through the people of Israel** who would act as a light to the world.

Deutero-Isaiah is known in particular for his teaching about the **Suffering Servant**, or the **Servant of Yahweh** (Isaiah 53), though we cannot be certain whether he was thinking of an individual or a certain community of people. Did he mean one person when he talked about the Servant, or the whole Jewish people? Or again, did he mean the remnant who would return to Jerusalem after the exile? It is useful to point out here that often in records relating to the religion of the Israelites, the community is pictured or spoken of as one person, so that it is not necessary to dwell too long on whether one person or the people as a whole are meant here. In any event, the idea of serving God was nothing new to the people of Israel, so that they could easily identify themselves with someone who would lead a life of suffering, undertaken for the sake of others and without complaint.

When Cyrus, the vassal king of the Elamite city of Anshan, rebelled in 550 BC, against Astyages and gained control of the Median empire and later took Babylon in 539 BC, he was hailed by Deutero-Isaiah as a deliverer of the Jewish people, and not just simply as a conqueror. **Isaiah believed that God was thus using Cyrus as an instrument of his goodness who would permit the Jews to return to their country in a way that would appear like a second exodus.** Cyrus' coming heralded the beginning of the Persian empire which lasted for two hundred years. He issued a decree allowing the Jews who so wished to return to their own country. Indeed, it was part of his general policy to send back to their homelands foreigners who had been carried away captive.

According to the book of Ezra (Ezra 1:2–4), the purpose of the return to Israel was specifically to rebuild the Temple. Cyrus certainly showed considerable sympathy for the religious susceptibilities of the Jewish people. Some forty-two thousand Jews are said to have returned with Sheshbazzar, a prince of Judah and son of Jehoiachin in 538 BC, although the actual figure may not have been as high. Many decided to stay in Babylon where, by then, they had established themselves in their own businesses. Those who did remain in Babylon seem to have assisted those who returned.

When the exiles reached Jerusalem, they found life there extremely difficult. The country had been ruled by Samaria in the absence of the Jewish leaders and new religious centres had been founded. When they began the task of rebuilding the city walls, they met the opposition of the Samaritans, though they did offer help with the rebuilding of the Temple. As the Samaritans were considered not to be of pure Jewish stock, having intermarried with non-Jews, their offer was declined.

More Jews returned to Jerusalem in 520 BC, with Zerubbabel, who succeeded Sheshbazzar, together with Joshua, a high priest. Assisted by the prophets Haggai and Zechariah, who urged them on, they rebuilt the Temple in 515 BC, though it was not as grand as the former magnificent Temple (Haggai 2:3). Zechariah referred to their leader Zerubbabel in terms which suggested that he could be the messiah, or anointed one, but it was Joshua, the high priest, who assumed a position of pre-eminence.

Isaiah chapters 56–66 contains yet other prophetic records which many scholars believe are somewhat later in date than the work of Deutero-Isaiah and which relate to the conditions in Judea soon after the return from exile (e.g. in Isaiah 56:7, the ruined Temple has been rebuilt). Perhaps a follower or followers of Deutero-Isaiah were continuing his prophetic work. He speaks of the oppression of the poor and the less fortunate and there is a general air of gloom about the times that he describes. These were early days after the return and the people needed effective leadership.

Nehemiah and Ezra

There is uncertainty regarding the dating of the arrival of Nehemiah and Ezra in Jerusalem. It is most probable, however, that Nehemiah arrived first in 444 BC, in the twentieth year of the reign of the Persian king, Artaxerxes I, (Nehemiah 2:1), and that Ezra the scribe followed in 397 BC, in the seventh year of the reign of Artaxerxes II (404–358 BC) (Ezra 7:7), rather than the opposite order, which might be supposed from the positioning of the books in the Old Testament. It is reasonable to suggest this order of events because Nehemiah set about repairing the walls of Jerusalem and in the time of Ezra they were already rebuilt. Furthermore, the general situation prevailing in the city on the arrival of Ezra would suggest a later date than that of Nehemiah.

We are told that **Nehemiah** was the cup-bearer to Artaxerxes at the royal court at Shushan and that he requested permission to return to Jerusalem so that he could help to **rebuild the walls of the city** (Nehemiah 2:1–10). He was not only allowed to return but was made governor of the province of Judah, which was thus freed from its ties to Samaria. On his arrival at Jerusalem, he decided to inspect the walls by night in case of opposition from the people of Samaria and from certain people who had remained in Jerusalem. Nehemiah eventually succeeded in organizing the rebuilding of the city walls despite the obstruction of Sanballat, the governor of Samaria, Tobiah, governor of the province of Ammon, which was beyond the river Jordan, and Geshem, governor of the province of Arabia, The people were divided into groups, with one group undertaking the rebuilding while another group stood on guard against attack. Nehemiah 6:15 states that the work was completed in under two months.

Nehemiah remained as governor of Judah for twelve years and during this time he **encouraged the Jews to improve their worship and their observance of the Law**. He returned to the Persian court and then made a second visit to Jerusalem to eradicate irreligious practices that had crept in and to encourage the people in the **strict observance of the sabbath**. The city gates were to be closed during the time of the Sabbath (Nehemiah 13:15–22), and only pure Jews were to be allowed into the Temple. Nehemiah was furious to find some children of mixed marriages could not even speak Hebrew. He subsequently **banned mixed marriages and ordered Jews to separate themselves from the practices and customs of other people**. Indeed, Nehemiah 9:2, points out how they were a people 'separated from all foreigners'.

Ezra, the priest and scribe (Ezra 7:21), arrived in Jerusalem with

53

the primary purpose of investigating the religious life of the people there and to **read the Law** to them.

> When the seventh month came, and the Israelites were now settled in their towns, the people assembled as one man in the square in front of the Water Gate, and Ezra the scribe was asked to bring the book of the law of Moses, which the Lord had enjoined upon Israel. On the first day of the seventh month, Ezra the priest brought the law before the assembly, every man and woman, and all who were capable of understanding what they heard. He read from it, facing the square in front of the Water Gate, from early morning till noon, in the presence of the men and the women, and those who could understand, all the people listened attentively to the book of the law. Ezra the scribe stood on a wooden platform for the purpose.
>
> (Nehemiah 8:1–4)

This 'Law' may have been the Pentateuch, that is, the first five books of the Old Testament, or parts of those books, but it is most likely that he read to them what is now Leviticus 17–26. This is known as the **Holiness Code.** In his address to the people **Ezra went further than Nehemiah on the strictness with which religious observances and rituals were to be kept**. Their religion, emphasized Ezra, must be pure. There was to be no slackening of the Jewish attitude towards non-Jews. Whereas Nehemiah had merely advocated that no further marriages should take place with non-Jews, Ezra **demanded that any Jew who had married a foreign woman should divorce her**. It appears that there were a few opponents to Ezra's words on the matter but we cannot be certain to what extent his ban was put into effect.

The Greek period of Jewish history

The Persian Empire came to an end with its defeat by Alexander the Great of Macedon, who ruled from 336 to 323 BC, and who achieved victory after victory in his military campaigns in Asia Minor, Syria, Persia and even as far as India. He encouraged the adoption of Greek thought, customs and culture in all these countries. On his death the generals fought for power. Around 300 BC, Ptolemy ruled in Egypt with Alexandria as his capital, and Seleucus ruled over most of Western Asia and Syria with two capitals: one on the Tigris and one at Antioch in Syria. Like Alexander, both Ptolemy and Seleucus encouraged the adoption of Hellenistic culture and language.

Palestine fell into the hands of Ptolemy in 301 BC, and remained under the rule of the Ptolemies until 198 BC. A series of high priests 'ruled' over the people there and these, in turn, were subject to their Ptolemaic overlords, The Jews were allowed to continue with their worship freely, even though Palestine became greatly influenced by Greek culture. The book entitled 'The Wisdom of Solomon', for example, was written by Greek-speaking Jews. During this period many Jews settled in Egypt. The **Septuagint** (Greek version of the Jewish scriptures) sometimes referred to as 'LXX', was written at Alexandria in Egypt. Jewish tradition has it that seventy (or seventy-two) scribes brought specially to Egypt from Jerusalem made the translation from Hebrew into Greek in seventy-two days. The work was completed, however, by various people over a number of years in the third century BC.

The situation in Palestine changed dramatically after 198 BC, when Ptolemy V was defeated by Antiochus III, or Antiochus the Great, as he was called, and the country came under the rule of the Seleucids, who governed there until 142 BC. While Antiochus III allowed the Jews freedom of worship, the attitude of Antiochus IV, called **Antiochus Epiphanes,** who ruled from 175 to 163 BC, was quite different. His love of Greek culture and religion prompted him to **set up an altar to the Greek god Zeus in the Temple at Jerusalem, and in 168 BC, he forbade any form of Jewish worship**. The books of the Maccabees in the Apocrypha give a graphic account of his reign. He is also mentioned in the book of Daniel, where he is called 'a contemptible person' (Daniel 11:21). Jews objected to the way in which he referred to himself as 'god manifest'. He banned the practice of circumcision, Sabbath observance and the celebrating of Jewish festivals. Jewish books were burnt, their very possession was prohibited, and all sacred vessels were removed from the Temple. Some Jews abandoned outward demonstration of their religion while others were tortured or killed for their faith.

In addition to religious harassment, **the Jews had to endure various intrigues during the reign of Antiochus Epiphanes regarding the position of high priest**. The high priest Onias III was a godly man whose principal concern was that the people should worship Yahweh without being tempted to introduce Hellenistic ideas. While absent from Jerusalem on one occasion, however, he was replaced by Joshua, his brother, who purposely changed his name to Jason, which was the Greek form of Joshua. Joshua obtained the position as the result of a bribe. Greek thought and culture was subsequently adopted on a large scale. Later a certain Menelaus replaced Jason, also gaining the position by means of a bribe.

The revolt of the Maccabees

The flagrantly anti-Jewish attitude of Antiochus Epiphanes soon enflamed the passions of the people. Mattathias, a priest from Modein, seventeen miles from Jerusalem, killed a Jew who was about to offer sacrifice to Zeus, together with a Greek officer who was overseeing the ceremony (I Maccabees 2:15–26). Mattathias and his five sons, Judas, John, Simon, Jonathan and Eleazar, then escaped to the neighbouring hills, where, together with many others, they planned rebellion against Antiochus. At first they would not fight on the sabbath until many hundreds of their number were killed. Mattathias then realized that to do God's work he would have to treat the sabbath like any other day, and fight on that day if necessary. On the death of his father in 166 BC, Judas took on the leadership of the rebels. He was often called 'the Hammerer'. He succeeded in destroying the altar to Zeus and by 164 BC had gained a certain degree of religious freedom for the people. Jonathan was made high priest in 141 BC, but was later murdered. Simon 'ruled' for ten relatively quiet years until he was murdered in 134 BC by his son-in-law. Simon's son, John Hyrcanus was made high priest in the same year and so began the Hasmonean dynasty of high-priest 'kings' which lasted until New Testament times.

Chapter 4
The Life and Teaching of Jesus Christ

The Synoptic Gospels

The word 'Synoptic' is used to refer to the first three books in the New Testament (Matthew, Mark and Luke) because they describe the life of Jesus from the same point of view. The authors of these books used similar material and wrote during the same period, that is, between AD 65 and AD 85. They used the words of eye-witnesses, and also oral material handed down and certain existing writings.

It is generally agreed that **Mark's Gospel was the first to be written** and can be dated about AD 65. The author was possibly the John Mark referred to in Acts 12:12, and he intended the book for a Christian Gentile community at Rome which was undergoing terrible persecution. Many leaders of the church in Rome were put to death at this time, including eye-witnesses of the ministry of Jesus and it became vital to commit the oral tradition to writing before it became lost or distorted. Mark's is the shortest of the four Gospels and is written in rather rough Greek but with great immediacy and vividness. It is likely that one of Mark's chief sources of information was the Apostle Peter who features very little in the narrative and whose shortcomings are very frankly portrayed. Matthew and Luke are thought to have written their Gospels around AD 85 and used material from Mark, together with their own material and also material from a source called Q, which stands for the German word *Quelle*, meaning 'source'. The existence of 'Q' is generally assumed because of some two hundred verses in Matthew which are very similar to verses which are in Luke but which are not included in Mark.

The interests of Matthew and Luke are very different. Luke may have been a Gentile doctor writing for Gentile Christians from Philippi in Greece or Troas in Asia Minor. About 65% of Mark's Gospel is in Luke. **Luke shows great interest in Jesus as the friend of the poor and the outcast**, and emphasizes the importance of **the Holy Spirit, prayer and forgiveness**. Luke stresses **Jesus' interest in Gentiles** and highlights the fact that the Gospel is good news for everyone and not just for the Jews. He also **gives a prominent place in his narrative to women**. Luke was probably the same person as the author of the Acts of the Apostles (Luke 1:1–4; Acts 1:1).

On the other hand little is known of **Matthew**, a Christian author who may have written from Antioch in Syria in about AD 85. He adopted about 95% of Mark's gospel, and **included many Old Testament references in his book to emphasize how Jesus was the fulfilment of Old Testament prophecy**.

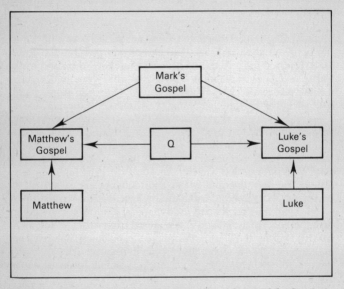

Figure 6. Diagram illustrating the interdependence of the Synoptic Gospels.

John's Gospel

John's Gospel is different from the other three and was written later, possibly about AD 100. The approach of the writer is **more**

Figure 7. Palestine in the time of Jesus (AD 30)

theological than historical. He may have been John the Elder, the author of the two letters John 2 and John 3, writing from Ephesus in Asia Minor.

The primary aim of the Gospel writers was not to compose an historical account of the life of Jesus. Their object was to record the life and work of Jesus as the Saviour of mankind. It is therefore impossible to be sure of the exact chronological order of some events in the life of Jesus.

The political background to the life of Jesus

Jesus was born a Jew in Palestine which had become part of the Roman Empire when it was conquered by Pompey in 63 BC. The Jews were very conscious of their unique status as the people of God and this made the rule of foreigners unbearable to them. The Romans were not only conquerors but pagans, and, according to the Jewish Law, unclean. Jewish nationalism expressed itself in violent uprisings which were harshly suppressed but soon flared up again. People longed for a messiah who would be an outstanding political and military figure. They wanted someone who would lead a rebellion against the Romans, driving them out of Palestine and restoring the country's independence.

Herod the Great ruled over the country as a vassal of Rome from 37 BC to 4 BC. At his suggestion, the country was divided on his death between his three sons. Archelaus was given Judea, Samaria and Idumea but proved too ambitious and was replaced by a Roman procurator in AD 6. Antipas was given Galilee and Perea, and Philip was given Iturea, which was the country north-east of the Sea of Galilee, together with Trachonitis.

The announcements of the birth of John the Baptist and of Jesus

The announcement of the birth of John the Baptist (Luke 1:5–25), took place during the reign of Herod the Great. Zechariah, a priest, whose wife Elizabeth was also from a priestly family, was performing his office at the Temple at Jerusalem, as every priest had to serve for a week twice each year. The angel Gabriel appeared to him and told him that he would have a son who would bring the people back to God's ways. He would be a Nazarite and touch no strong drink, thus indicating that his life would be dedicated to God. Zechariah was instructed to call the boy John, which means 'God has been gracious'. Because Zechariah could not believe the vision he was struck dumb and did not recover his speech until the naming of the child.

The announcement of the conception of Jesus was similarly given to Mary at Nazareth by the angel Gabriel (Luke 1:26–38; Matthew 1:18–25). Mary was betrothed to Joseph and would be expected to marry him within a year. The belief in a virgin birth was not unusual in world religions and it has often been introduced to suggest the appearance or work of God. It is suggested that Elizabeth and Mary were related, but how is not certain; perhaps Elizabeth was Mary's aunt. Luke tells us (Luke 1:39–45), that the two met in a town of Judah. The Magnificat, the Song of Praise sung by Mary when Elizabeth greeted her (Luke 1:46–56), is based on the Song of Hannah (I Samuel 2:1–10).

The birth of John the Baptist and the birth of Jesus

Elizabeth had a son as prophesied by the angel and he was duly called John (Luke 1:62–63). When he was eight days old he was circumcised according to Jewish law (Leviticus 12:3). In his Song of Praise to God, called the Benedictus (Luke 1:68–79), Zechariah refers to John as the forerunner of the Lord, repeating the words of the angel Gabriel.

The birth of Jesus (Luke 2:1–20), took place during the reign of the emperor Augustus at the time of a census which involved Joseph and Mary travelling from Nazareth in Galilee to Bethlehem in Judea. The journey was necessary because Joseph was a descendant of David who came from Bethlehem and it was here that Jesus was born.

Luke tells us that shepherds visited Jesus to worship him (Luke 2:16–18). Matthew describes a visit of astrologers, or 'magi', from the east (Matthew 2:1–12). These were probably Persians or Arabians and followers of Zoroaster who may have come from

Babylon, the astrological centre. They had followed a star, believing that it would take them to the messiah they were expecting. They brought gifts with them: gold, as a symbol of kingship, frankincense, a symbol of worship and hence holiness, and myrrh, a symbol of suffering.

The presentation of Jesus in the Temple

Jesus' parents brought him to the Temple for circumcision and to present a gift to the priests in thanksgiving. They were greeted by a devout Jew called Simeon, who announced that God's promise had been fulfilled in Jesus. Anna, an aged prophetess, similarly greeted the child and thanked God for him. The family then returned to Nazareth where Jesus grew up.

The boyhood visit to the Temple

Only Luke records a visit made by Jesus and his parents to the Temple when he was twelve (Luke 2:41–52). It was customary for Jews to attend the Temple three times a year for the Pilgrim festivals of Passover, Pentecost and Tabernacles (Exodus 23:14–17), though if long distances were involved it was acceptable for them to attend for just the Passover festival. Suddenly, on the journey home, Jesus' parents realised that he was missing. They returned to the Temple and found him listening to and discussing with the rabbis. Apart from this, all we learn of Jesus' early life is that he 'advanced in wisdom and in favour with God and men' (Luke 2:52).

The message of John the Baptist

According to Luke, John preached a 'baptism of repentance' to the people of the Jordan valley during the reign of the emperor Tiberius, that is, about AD 28–29. He urged them to repent and be baptized because the kingdom of heaven was close at hand and the coming of the messiah was imminent. This baptism entailed a ritual washing in the River Jordan to indicate publicly that by their sin they had failed God. The people, he said, should repent before the coming judgment which would affect Jews as well as unbelievers. He spoke harsh words and, dressed in the habit of an ascetic, appeared to the people like a prophet from Old Testament times. By some he was regarded as the new Elijah. He prepared the way for the one who would baptize them with the Holy Spirit. John denied that he was the messiah but declared that the messiah was one who already stood among them, whose shoes he was not worthy to unloose (removing a guest's shoes was the work of a humble servant).

John's ethical teaching is contained in Luke 3:10–14. The common people were instructed to share what they had with those in need, tax-gatherers were not to take more than they were entitled to, and soldiers were urged to desist from blackmail and intimidation and told to be content with their wages. Later, Herod Antipas put John in prison for criticizing his marriage to his brother's wife, Herodias.

The baptism of Jesus

The record of Jesus' baptism by John when he was about thirty years of age was probably handed down orally from Jesus himself. John was extremely reluctant to baptize him, but Jesus insisted, wishing to identify himself with the people of Israel whom John had called to repentance. We are told that, when Jesus was baptized, heaven opened, the Holy Spirit descended on him in the form of a dove, and the voice of God spoke from heaven. This may have been experienced only by Jesus or have been witnessed by others too. Jesus obviously saw himself as having a very special rôle to play at this stage, as the quotations from Psalm 2:7 and Isaiah 42 :1 (which is from part of one of the Servant Songs) illustrated.

The temptation of Jesus

Immediately after his baptism, Jesus spent a period of forty days fasting alone in the wilderness somewhere near the Dead Sea and during this time he was tempted by the devil. The reference to forty days is possibly intended to remind readers of the forty years that the Israelites spent in the desert. Once again, the source of the account was probably Jesus himself. At that time there were many popular ideas about a revolutionary figure who would deliver the people from the Romans and Jesus wanted to be alone to consider and pray about what kind of messiah he was going to be. According to Luke's Gospel the three temptations took place in the following order. Jesus was first **tempted to turn stones into bread**. He knew, however, that what the people needed was spiritual food and quoted Deuteronomy 8:3 at the devil, 'Man cannot live on bread alone.' Then **the devil told him that he could have all the kingdoms of the world if he worshipped him**. In response Jesus quoted Deuteronomy 6:13: 'You shall fear the Lord your God, serve him alone.' Finally the devil **tempted Jesus to throw himself down from the pinnacle of the Temple** so as to win over the people. Jesus could see no value in such a dramatic gesture and quoted again from the Old Testament, this time Deuteronomy 6:16 'You must not challenge the Lord your God'. After this the devil left him.

Jesus' early work in Galilee and the appointment of the disciples

After Jesus' temptations he returned to Galilee. When he arrived at Nazareth, his home town, he went to the synagogue where he was invited to read the lesson (Luke 4:16–30). He read from the scroll of Isaiah 58:6 and 61:1–2:

> The spirit of the Lord is upon me; because the Lord has anointed me; he has sent me to bring good news to the humble, to bind up the broken-hearted, to proclaim liberty to captives and release to those in prison; to proclaim a year of the Lord's favour.

He declared that the scriptures had been fulfilled that day in him, so implying that he would somehow inaugurate a new age. At this stage the people became intensely angry and threw him out of the town. According to the Gospels Jesus never returned to Nazareth.

At Capernaum Jesus preached in the local synagogue with more success than at Nazareth and began his ministry of healing. Finding a need for assistants, he appointed men to proclaim the coming of the kingdom of God. **Peter, James and John** were called first, according to Luke (Luke 5:1–11), and others followed (Luke 6:12–16): **Andrew, Philip, Bartholomew, Matthew, Thomas, James** the son of Alphaeus, Simon who was called the Zealot, Judas the son of James, and Judas Iscariot, though the list of the twelve varies according to which Gospel is being read. All but one, Judas, were from Galilee, and he came from Judea. Very likely Jesus had the twelve tribes of Israel in mind when he chose twelve disciples. Later the Twelve were commissioned and sent out to preach about the kingdom and to heal the sick (Luke 9:1–6). Luke also records the occasion when Jesus sent out seventy men in pairs to preach and heal people (Luke 10:1–16). It is thought by some that this is a duplicate of the account in Luke 9:1–6.

From the early days of Jesus' work in Galilee he may well have **come into conflict with the Jewish authorities**. Luke has collected accounts of these incidents, such as:

1. The healing of a paralytic (Luke 5:17–16)   In this account, a paralysed man was brought by his friends to Jesus for healing and lowered through the roof of the house where he was staying because it was too crowded to get in by any other way. Jesus told the man his sins were forgiven. **The Pharisees were infuriated at the idea that Jesus could forgive sins**. Such talk, they said, was blasphemous as only God could do this. Nevertheless, the man was healed. It is interesting to note that Jesus uses the title **'Son of Man'** here for the first time in the Gospels to refer to himself.

2. The call of Levi (Luke 5:27–32)   Jesus upset the Pharisees further by eating at the house of Levi, a tax collector. Most Jews despised those of that calling, the more so as it supported the hated Roman regime. Jesus' prompt response was that he came to call precisely such people to repentance.

3. A question about fasting (Luke 5:33–35)   Jesus' critics complained that, unlike John's disciples, **his followers did not observe the usual custom of fasting**. Jesus made a comparison with a wedding celebration and, perhaps looking to his own future, declared that it was appropriate for friends to celebrate while the bridegroom was still with them.

4. An incident in the cornfields (Luke 6:1–5)   This is the first of a number of occasions when **Jesus was criticized for 'working' on the sabbath**. According to Exodus 20:10, no Jew was allowed to work on the day of rest. The Pharisees had complained that as Jesus' disciples passed through some cornfields, they plucked the ears of corn, rubbed them in their hands and ate them. Such an action was regarded as work and therefore indefensible on the sabbath. Jesus replied by pointing out that when King David was fleeing from his pursuers he had eaten the sacred bread from the house of God which only the priests were allowed to eat and had not been rebuked, though in fact this incident did not take place on the sabbath. **Jesus implied that human needs were more important than the Law. The Son of Man was Lord of the sabbath.**

5. The healing of a man's withered hand (Luke 6:6–11) This incident took place on another Sabbath. It was only permissible to heal someone on the Sabbath if the person's life was in danger and the Pharisees were angry with Jesus for healing the man.

Further 'conflict' stories can be found in Luke 13:10–17, with the account of the **infirm woman**, and the **man with dropsy** (Luke 14:1–6).

Jesus' miracles

All of the Gospels refer to miracles performed by Jesus during his ministry. Many of these can be found at the beginning of Luke's Gospel, such as the following:

1. The healing of the centurian's servant (Luke 7:1–10) This took place at Capernaum and concerned a Gentile. It demonstrates a soldier's great faith. The healing took place without Jesus even seeing the servant and **shows clearly Jesus was concerned for Gentiles as well as Jews.**

2. The raising of the widow's son (Luke 7:11–17) This incident (recorded only in Luke) took place at a village in Galilee called Nain, which was about twenty-five miles from Capernaum. As Jesus approached the village, he met a funeral cortège. Having compassion on a woman whose son had died, he touched the bier (which the Pharisees would have considered unclean) and told the young man to get up. **This and the story of Jairus' daughter are the only raisings of the dead recorded in the Synoptic Gospels.** John in his Gospel provides the account of the raising of Lazarus.

3. The storm on the Lake (Luke 8:22–25) **This is one of the few nature miracles recorded by the Synoptic Gospel writers.** Storms were frequent occurrences on the Lake of Galilee and on this occasion Jesus was with his disciples in a boat in danger of sinking. He rebuked the wind and the water and demonstrated his power over the forces of nature.

4. The Gadarene madman (Luke 8:26–39) The country of Gadara was located somewhere on the eastern side of Lake Galilee. There Jesus met a man possessed by devils who addressed him as 'Son of the Most High God'. He may have been referring to Jesus as the messiah or simply as a follower of the God of the Jews. The man was called Legion because he was possessed by so many devils. Jesus cast the devils out of the man, thus restoring him to his right mind and sent them into a herd of pigs which promptly rushed into the lake and drowned. **In this miracle Jesus demonstrated his authority over demonic powers.**

5. Jairus' daughter (Luke 8:40–42, 49–56) Jairus was evidently an elder of the synagogue whose daughter was dying. He came to Jesus, asking him to heal her, but by the time they reached the house, the girl was already dead. Declaring that she was only asleep, Jesus took her by the hand and told her to get up. **This incident again shows Jesus' authority even over death.**

6. The feeding of the five thousand (Luke 9:10–17) This is another of Jesus' nature miracles. He was in the country near Bethsaida with his disciples, preaching and healing. About five thousand people had come to hear Jesus preach and by the evening they were hungry. They were told to sit down in groups of fifty, and five loaves and two fishes were found to be sufficient to feed them all. Indeed, Luke says that they all ate 'to their hearts' content', and that the scraps filled twelve 'great' baskets (Luke 9:17). It is possible that each group of people shared the food that they brought, or, alternatively, that the number of people present was greatly exaggerated. This is possible in so far as the disciples did not seem to be at all surprised at the way in which the food went round. This miracle is also recorded by the other Gospel writers (Matthew 14:13–21; Mark 6:30–44; John 6:1–14). Matthew and Mark describe an occasion on which four thousand people were miraculously fed, which may be simply a further account of this incident.

All of these miracles were regarded as signs of God's power

administered through acts of Jesus. They prompted John the Baptist to send two of his disciples to Jesus with a message asking if he was the one who was to come, meaning the messiah, or whether they should look for another (Luke 7:18–23). By the way he spoke of the miracles he performed Jesus certainly implied that he was the messiah.

According to the Jewish historian, Josephus, John the Baptist was held in a fortress on the eastern side of the Dead Sea and it was from here that he sent his disciples to Jesus. Clearly, John was not sure whether Jesus was the messiah and what rôle he was to play. Jesus' reply was decisive, however: ' "Go," he said, "and tell John what you have seen and heard: how the blind recover their sight, the lame walk, the lepers are made clean, the deaf hear, the dead are raised to life, the poor are hearing the good news." ' (Luke 7:22).

John the Baptist was nearing the end of his life and his work was at an end. Matthew 14:3–12 and Mark 6:17–29 record his death by execution on the orders of Herod. Having promised his wife Herodias anything she wanted on the event of his birthday, he could not go back on his word. Herodias hated John because of his condemnation of her marriage to Herod and so she asked for his head! Yet John died in the knowledge that his work was being continued by one mightier than he was. He had acted as the herald and the messiah would follow.

The Pharisees and the Sadducees

The **Pharisees** came into existence about the middle of the second century BC. The word 'Pharisee' means 'the separated ones', as they **kept themselves apart from the Gentiles** and their ways. They **observed the written Law**, or Torah, and **also the Oral Law**, or the Tradition of the elders. The latter consisted of supplements to the written Law that had been made over a period of years. The Pharisees **believed in a resurrection, in a place called Hades**, which they envisaged as a rather gloomy abode for the dead, and in a **final judgment**. They also looked forward to the **coming of a messiah. They amassed a series of laws to cover every aspect of life**.

Jesus came into collision with the Pharisees on several occasions, as related in the conflict stories and also when they asked Jesus for a sign, which he refused to give. **Jesus warned his followers of the Pharisees in no uncertain terms** (Luke 11:37–54; Matthew 23:1–36), condemning their self-righteousness, by which God was not deceived. The account of the Pharisees and the tax-collector (Luke 18:9–14), is a parable about a right relationship with God.

The **Sadducees** were probably so called after Zadok, a priest, who lived in the reign of Solomon (I Kings 1:39). They formed the party of the **leading priests** and the **lay aristocracy** of Jesus' time and were likely to be **leaders of the Sanhedrin**, the Jewish Council. They **observed only the written Law of Moses**, that is the first five books of the Old Testament, and so **did not believe in a resurrection**. For this reason it was they who questioned Jesus and attempted to trap him when discussing the after-life. They found that it was not in their interest to resist the Roman government, since their position as the aristocracy would probably have suffered and they knew that the Jewish nation would also suffer.

The Zealots

We should note here that, at the time of Jesus, there was an extreme fanatical religious party called the Zealots. The movement began with Judas of Galilee in AD 6 (not Judas Iscariot), and a rebellion in AD 65. The Zealots **attempted to initiate a rule of God on earth by using force**. They hated the Romans and sought every means to be rid of them. They had no room for compromise.

The Essenes

In contrast to the Zealots, the Essenes, or 'pious ones', devoted themselves to **serve God in a peaceful manner, leading a life of prayer and contemplation**. It has been claimed that John the Baptist may have been an Essene. They were based in a monastery by the Dead Sea and lived a communal life, working together and sharing all their possessions. They may have been responsible for the writing of the Dead Sea scrolls which were found in a cave by the Dead Sea in 1947. These contain many writings from the Old Testament and other Jewish writings.

The Sermon (best known as the Sermon on the Mount)
This is a collection of Jesus' teachings on a variety of topics, not all of which were spoken on the same occasion. Matthew's Sermon on the Mount (Matthew 5–7), is very similar to Luke's Sermon on the Plain (Luke 6:17–49), and they both probably took their common material from Q. Both begin with the **'Beatitudes'**, or blessings, which describe **the qualities of those who would be members of the kingdom of God.** They are all other-worldly in approach. The phrase 'How blest' bears the meaning 'How happy are . . .' In his version, Luke adds 'Woes' which represent the negative aspect of the Beatitudes. Matthew refers to:

1. The poor in spirit   These are those who realize they are poor in a spiritual sense and know that they need God's grace. Such people are truly blest and have the humility that comes from an appreciation of God's grace.

2. Those that mourn   These people grieve for their own sins and those of mankind.

3. The meek   Like those mentioned in the first Beatitude, these people have the grace that comes from humility. They are unassuming and do not stand on their rights. This does not mean that they are weak or necessarily submissive. Their strength and confidence is not in themselves, but in God.

4. Those who hunger and thirst for righteousness   These are those who long for God's rule on earth and desire that his will shall be done in their own lives as well as in society.

5. The merciful   These are the forgiving.

6. The pure in heart   These people are single-minded in their service of God. Their thoughts are pure and they do not readily attribute evil motives to others.

7. The peacemakers   These are those who yearn and strive for peace in the world and who have peace within themselves because of their trust in God.

8. Those who suffer for righteousness' sake   These endure persecution bravely because of their loyalty to God. They are in the company of all the prophets and servants of God who have suffered in the past.

The followers of Jesus are to be like lights shining in the darkness. They are to be known for their good works (Matthew 5:13–16). **They must go further than the Jewish Law commands.** For example, they

70

must not even harbour thoughts of hatred, let alone commit murder (Matthew 5:21–26). Indeed, they are to love their enemies (Matthew 5:38–48). Far from committing adultery, a man must not even look at a woman lustfully (Matthew 5:27–30). Jesus stressed the point that **it is a person's inner thoughts which really matter**. He was equally emphatic about divorce and remarriage which he opposed, except in the case of immorality (Matthew 5:31–32). There should be **no limit to one's goodness**. In their almsgiving (Matthew 6:1–4), their prayers (Matthew 6:5–15), and their fasting (Matthew 6:16–18), the **followers of Jesus are to act with sincerity and without show**. Jesus gave the **Lord's Prayer** as a guide to prayer.

The principal concern of the followers of Jesus at all times should be about spiritual matters. They should not be anxious about anything (Matthew 6:25, 33, and 34). **They must not judge others without first assessing their own behaviour**. It is for God alone to judge others. The 'Golden Rule' (Matthew 7:12), should be one's guide, the standard to live by: 'Always treat others as you would like them to treat you; that is the Law and the prophets'. Everyone should act like the man who built his house on a rock, a firm foundation. True followers of Jesus should base their whole lives on his teachings.

The parables of Jesus

As he travelled round the towns and villages of Galilee, Jesus often used parables to give colour and force to his teachings. He spoke to the people wherever he could, on a hill or by a lake, since he could not now preach in the synagogues.

Jesus used parables to describe the kingdom of God, as the following examples will illustrate:
1. The parable of the sower (Luke 8:4–8, 11–15), is really concerned with Jesus' whole mission on earth. It is generally assumed that the sower in this (verses 11–15) represents a Christian teacher rather than Jesus himself. Those who hear the word of God and understand it and act upon it are compared with good soil where the seed can take root and grow. The seeds that fall on the pathway represent the gospel being preached to those whose minds are closed, and the stony ground stands for those who

71

receive the message gladly but ultimately find such difficulty with Jesus' teaching that they reject it. The thistles or thorns represent worldly cares and preoccupations which may smother people's initial interest in and enthusiasm for the gospel. There is the implication in the parable that the kingdom had already come.

2. The parable of the lamp (Luke 8:16–18) shows how the truth of Jesus' words would be seen by everyone.

3. The parable of the seed growing secretly (Mark 4:26–29), emphasizes how the kingdom will grow and develop of its own accord.

4. The parable of the mustard seed (Luke 13:18–19), suggests that as one small seed can grow into a large tree so will God's kingdom increase in size.

5. The parable of the leaven (Luke 13:20–21), illustrates the power of the kingdom. It will grow in size just as a loaf rises when leavened.

6. The parables of the treasure and pearl merchant (Matthew 13:44–46) Here the kingdom is compared to hidden treasure or a pearl that a man will sell all that he has, to possess, Jesus encouraged the idea of a person having the greatest enthusiasm about the kingdom. It was worthwhile giving up everything to gain entry into the kingdom.

7. The parable of the net full of fishes (Matthew 13:47–50) compares the kingdom to a net which picks up all sorts of things, good and bad. Jesus suggested that not all those who hear about the kingdom are worthy of it. God will judge who is worthy and who is not. It has been suggested that perhaps Jesus was thinking here of himself and his disciples as fishers of men who encountered all sorts of people on their missions.

Luke in his Gospel shows how Jesus was always concerned with the lost, as three parables in particular demonstrate. When the Pharisees complained that Jesus was entertaining sinners, Jesus replied with the **parable of the lost sheep** and asked them if they would not go and search for one lost sheep out of a hundred, leaving the ninety-nine who were safe in the fold, (Luke 15:1–7). He compared the lost sheep with the one sinner who repented. Jesus was thinking of God as the Shepherd of Israel. Similarly he spoke of a **lost coin** (Luke 15:8–10), which a woman searched the whole house to find. Like the lost sheep, it was worth seeking and in just such a way God seeks after sinners. The **parable of the lost son (Luke 15:11–32)**, otherwise known as the **prodigal son**, demonstrates God's love for his people. It tells of a man with two sons, one of whom took his share of the estate, squandered it all and when quite destitute repented and returned home to the great delight of his father. The elder brother, who was annoyed with his father for welcoming back the son, represents the Pharisees and the younger one represents the sinners of the world.

The **parable of the pounds** (Luke 19:11–27); the **parable of the dishonest steward** (Luke 16:1–13); and the **parable of Dives and Lazarus** (Luke 16:19–31), are included only in Luke.

Peter's confession of faith at Caesarea Philippi
(Luke 9:18–27; Matthew 16:13–28; Mark 8:27–9:1)

One day when Jesus and his disciples were near Caesarea Philippi, in Herod Philip's territory, about twenty-four miles north of the Sea of Galilee, an event occurred which marked an important turning-point in the disciples' understanding of Jesus. Jesus questioned them regarding their inner thoughts about the purpose of his work and mission. 'Who do the people say that I am?', he asked them. John the Baptist, or Elijah, or one of the prophets, was the reply. Jesus, however, was more interested in knowing who his disciples thought he was. Peter was the first to reply, proclaiming that **Jesus was God's messiah** (Luke 9:21) This was the first time, according to the Gospel records, that Jesus was openly called the messiah, and he immediately **instructed his disciples to tell no one**. Matthew, in contrast to Mark and Luke, has an additional reference to Peter as the rock on which Jesus would build his church. Referring to himself as the Son of Man, Jesus told his disciples that **he must go to Jerusalem and suffer death there. He would then be raised again on the third day**. We find Jesus' prediction of his death in Luke 9:44 and 18:31–34, as well as in the other Gospel parallels.

Having predicted his death, Jesus pointed out how difficult it was to be a true follower of his (Luke 9:23–24): 'If anyone wishes to be a follower of mine, he must leave self behind; day after day he must take up his cross, and come with me. Whoever cares for his own safety is lost; but if a man will let himself be lost for my sake, that man is safe.' The commitment must be total on their part.

73

They could hold back nothing of themselves, even their parents or friends. Such were the demands of faith in him. Following Jesus was to affect their whole lives; no other response was possible.

Jesus is transfigured (Luke 9:28–36; Matthew 17:1–13, Mark 9:2–13)

A short while later, Jesus was on a mountain with Peter, James and John, praying. This was probably Mount Hermon, which was fourteen miles north of Caesarea Philippi. The text tells us that the appearance of Jesus' face changed and his clothes became dazzling white. The disciples saw two men, identified as Moses and Elijah, standing with Jesus. Clearly, in their minds, the disciples saw Jesus continuing and fulfilling the work of these two famous leaders from the Old Testament who represented the Law and the prophets. As they watched, a cloud came down and they heard the words of God: 'This is my Son, my Chosen; listen to him', words very similar to those spoken at Jesus' baptism.

The incident reminds us of the transfiguration of Moses which is recorded in the book of Exodus (Exodus 34:29–35): when Moses received the Ten Commandments, his face shone so brightly that the people could not look at him when he came down from the presence of God. The cloud that overshadowed those on the Mount of Transfiguration was a symbol of the presence of God, like the cloud which led the Israelites through the wilderness. Peter even suggested that they made three booths, or shelters, for Jesus, Moses and Elijah, like the shelters used by their ancestors (Leviticus 23:42–43). According to Luke, Moses and Elijah spoke with Jesus of his coming 'departure'—a translation of the word 'exodus' in the original Greek. The word suggests that what was to happen at Jerusalem would be a new 'exodus': Jesus' death and resurrection were to be the spiritual counterpart of the deliverance of Israel from slavery, for by them people would be saved from slavery to sin. Once again the disciples remained silent about what they had seen.

The journey to Jerusalem

Jesus made a firm decision to go to Jerusalem and set out via Samaria, preaching and healing on the way. At one Samaritan village in particular he was not welcome because he made it known that he was heading for Jerusalem, the Jewish capital (Luke 9:51–56). This was because Jews and Samaritans refused to have any dealings with one another. The Jews hated the Samaritans because they had inter-married with other races after the Assyrian invasion of Israel in the eighth century BC and had not maintained their racial and religious purity. The Samaritans, for their part, hated the Jews. Luke tells us that, despite this traditional hostility, Jesus healed ten lepers as he travelled through the borders of Samaria and Galilee and only a Samaritan gave him thanks (Luke 17:11–19).

On their way to Jerusalem the disciples had many discussions with Jesus about his work and mission. It appears that **they still did not understand the true nature of Jesus' messiahship**, as indicated by James' and John's request to Jesus for the two places of honour, one on each side of him in the kingdom that was to come (Mark 10:35–45; Matthew 20:20–28). They clearly expected a visible rule of God on earth, in spite of Jesus' warning of his sufferings to come. Jesus rebuked the disciples, saying that **the Son of Man came not to be served but to serve**. In Luke we find an emphasis on the importance of serving others (Luke 17:7–10). **None of the disciples, Jesus said, was greater than the others** (Luke 9:46). They must all be humble and receive the kingdom like a child (Luke 18:17). The cost of being a disciple would involve much more than they thought. Many would fail. Would-be followers must make an immediate decision (Luke 9:57–62). Furthermore, a follower must be prepared to take up his cross and follow Jesus (Luke 14:27).

The entry into Jerusalem
(Luke 19:28–44); Matthew 21:1–9; Mark 11:1–11; John 12:12–19)
When Jesus and the disciples were approaching Jerusalem he sent two of them to a village to collect a colt. Evidently Jesus had already made the necessary arrangements. They entered the city from the Mount of Olives, and according to Luke, the disciples sang a passage from Psalm 118:26: 'Blessed in the name of the Lord are all who come', which was originally the priest's blessing

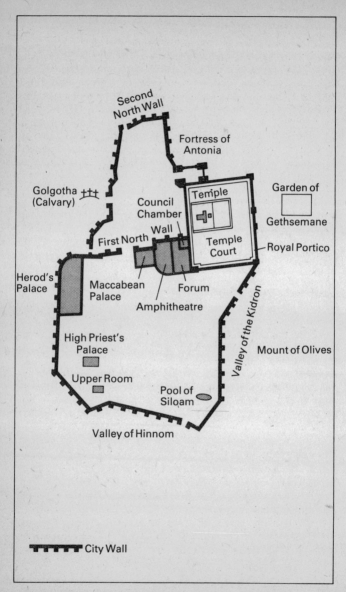

Figure 8. Jerusalem in the time of Jesus

pronounced on pilgrims coming up to the Temple for a festival. John's Gospel provides a more dramatic description. There the 'great body of pilgrims' greeted Jesus with palm branches. It is this occasion that has given us the name 'Palm Sunday'. Matthew adds the reference to Jesus as a king riding on an ass (Zechariah 9:9).

Later that day or possibly the next day, **Jesus entered the Temple at Jerusalem (Luke 19:45–48), and drove out the traders and money-changers**, quoting Isaiah 56:7 and Jeremiah 7:11 as he did so. The stalls were probably in the Court of the Gentiles. Afterwards, Jesus taught in the Temple over a period of days and healed the sick. This aroused the hostility of the chief priests and lawyers but they were powerless to stop him because of the support that he received from the ordinary people.

Discussions with the Pharisees and Sadducees—Judas plans to betray Jesus

The priests, lawyers and elders, who would have been members of the Sanhedrin, **asked Jesus by what authority he preached and healed the sick** (Luke 20:1–8). He responded by asking them by what authority John the Baptist had performed his work. To this they would give no answer.

In an attempt to trap him, **scribes and chief priests asked whether it was lawful for them to pay taxes to the Roman emperor** (Luke 20:19–26). Jesus replied by saying that as they received benefits from Rome, they owed payments to Rome, and so also as they received benefits from God, so must payment be made to God.

Later **the Sadducees asked him a question about the resurrection** (Luke 20:27–40). A man had died childless, and so, according to Jewish law (Deuteronomy 25:5–10), his brother married the widow, then he, too, died childless. In all, seven brothers married the woman and all died childless. The Sadducees asked him whose wife she would be at the resurrection. In his reply Jesus rebuked the Sadducees for their line of reasoning and told them that marriage is for this life only, for the next life is of a spiritual nature.

Finding it so difficult to trap Jesus, the chief priests planned to arrest him by some means. Their opportunity came when Judas offered to betray him (Luke 22:3–6). The reason for the betrayal is not known. It is possible that Judas was disappointed that Jesus was not adopting a revolutionary approach to his messianic mission.

The Last Supper and the arrest of Jesus
(Luke 22:7–61; Matthew 26:17–56 and 69–75; Mark 14:12–52)

Jesus sent Peter and John into Jerusalem to prepare for the Passover in an upper room. According to John's Gospel, this meal took place on the evening before the Passover. This was the festival at which the Jews commemorated their deliverance from Egypt but gave thanks also for all God's blessings to his people including the covenant and the inheritance of the Promised Land. During the meal Jesus **blessed and broke the bread**, giving some to his disciples and saying: **'Take this and eat; this is my body.'** He took a **cup of wine** and, after blessing it, gave it to them, saying: **'Drink from it, all of you. For this is my blood, the blood of the covenant, shed for many for the forgiveness of sins.'** (Matthew 26:26–28)

Body and blood together represent life, so Jesus, was, in effect, telling his disciples that he was to give his life for them. He was using the language of sacrifice–the breaking of the bread and the pouring out of the wine symbolized his death. The covenant represented a **new relationship between God and his followers**, taking the place of the old covenant between God and the people in the time of Moses. The old covenant had failed because the people were unable to keep their part of the agreement and the Old Testament in the Bible gives us a record of their failure. According to the prophet Jeremiah, God had revealed that there would one day be a new covenant, (Jeremiah 31:31–34); 'I will set my law within them and write it on their hearts'. Jesus said that this new covenant was being inaugurated at the Last Supper and would be sealed by his blood on Calvary.

Even at this stage some of the disciples were arguing among themselves about who ranked the highest. When Peter said he would go with Jesus to prison and death, Jesus told him that,

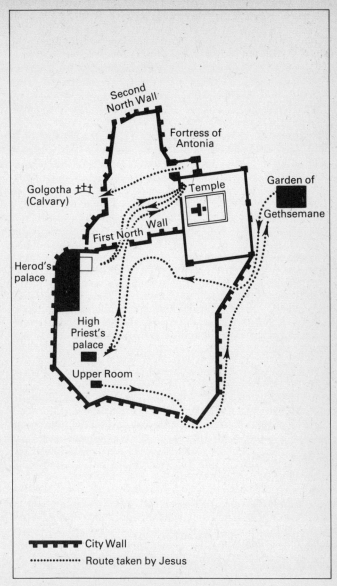

Figure 9. Route taken by Jesus on the last night in Jerusalem

before the night was through, he would deny him three times. The actual denials are recorded in Luke 22:54–61. Later, Jesus and the disciples went to the Mount of Olives to pray. It was at this point that Judas arrived with a crowd of people 'armed with swords and cudgels' to arrest Jesus (Matthew 26:47).

The trials of Jesus (Luke 22:66–71; 23:1–25; Matthew 26:57–68; 27:1–31; Mark 14:53–65; John 18:19–19:16)

All four Gospels have records of the trials of Jesus and refer in total to six occasions when Jesus appeared before the authorities: before Annas, father-in-law of the high priest, Caiaphas; before Caiaphas; before the full Sanhedrin; before Pontius Pilate; before Herod Antipas; and then before Pilate again. The reasons for seeking Jesus' death were probably:

1. the challenging of their authority, most recently in the cleansing of the Temple;
2. Jesus' attitude to the Jewish Law, and especially Sabbath observance;
3. the danger of a popular rising against the Romans as a result of his claim to be the messiah. If the chief priests were not seen to take action on a case of treason, this would endanger the privileged position granted them by the Romans.

It is most unlikely that all of these were formal trials. Probably the Roman trial before Pilate was the only one that was official. Jesus' appearances before members of the Sanhedrin were interrogations rather than trials, especially since it was not legal to hold a trial at night. False witnesses were brought forward but their evidence did not agree. Eventually two came forward and accused Jesus of wanting to destroy the Temple. This amounted to a charge of blasphemy, but should have been inadmissable because what they said was not only inaccurate but contradictory. Throughout all this Jesus remained silent. Finally he was asked directly if he was the messiah, to which he replied that he was. He was accused first of blasphemy but later the more serious accusation of treason was directed at him as his claim to be the messiah constituted a challenge to the Roman authorities and even to Caesar himself. The charge brought against Jesus at the trial before Pilate was that of treason. It must be noted that these 'trials' departed from established procedure on several points:

1. Although the Sanhedrin was, in theory, entitled to sit at night it could not pass sentence of death then.
2. A false witness always suffered the penalty which would have been awarded to the innocent victim.
3. If there was a unanimous verdict of guilty it was compulsory to delay the sentence for twenty four hours.
4. The correct procedure was to make a charge and call witnesses rather than questioning a prisoner in the hope that he would condemn himself.
5. The beating of a prisoner at a trial was most irregular.
6. If witnesses disagreed, a trial was supposed to end.

Responsibility for passing sentence fell on Pilate, though he was unwilling to condemn Jesus to death. There seems little doubt, at least according to Luke's Gospel, that Pontius Pilate wanted to release Jesus. He would have been content to give him a flogging, then set him free. It is likely that supporters of Barabbas were on the scene as well as members of the Sanhedrin and these all made the situation difficult for Pilate. Matthew's Gospel (Matthew 27:19, 24–25), tells us about Pilate's wife who sent her husband a special message about Jesus while the trial was in progress: 'Have nothing to do with that innocent man; I was much troubled on his account in my dreams last night'. No doubt she and Pilate were disturbed by the prospect of the sentence of death being passed on Jesus. But any possible alternative was not to be. The crowd demanded Jesus' life and the release of Barabbas, who had initiated a local uprising. It may have been a local custom to release a prisoner at certain times of the year, especially at the time of a festival. Barabbas was accordingly freed. Overcome with remorse, Judas returned the payment for his treachery to the priests and then hanged himself (Matthew 27:3–10).

The Crucifixion and death of Jesus
(Luke 23:26–43; Matthew 27:32–54; Mark 15:21–39; John 19:17–37)
Jesus was flogged and mocked by the soldiers, who dressed him in a robe of royal purple, placed on his head a crown of thorns as a substitute for the laurel wreath worn by emperors and taunted

him with 'Hail, King of the Jews' He was then taken out to the place of execution. It was customary for a condemned man to carry the cross-beam of the cross, but in Jesus' case, a man called Simon from Cyrene in North Africa was charged with the task of carrying it. Outside the city, at a place called 'the Skull', known as **Golgotha** by the Jews and **Calvary** by the Romans, Jesus was placed on a cross alongside two condemned criminals. Above his head was placed a sign which read 'Jesus of Nazareth, the King of the Jews'. The nailing up of a titulus or notice stating the crime of the prisoner was common practice. The description of Jesus as 'King of the Jews' may have been a deliberate insult to the Jews on the part of Pilate. Some women of Jerusalem provided drugged wine to ease the pain of crucifixion. This was permitted by the Romans but Jesus refused it. The mocking soldiers nearby divided his clothes among them by casting lots. Passers-by and the chief priests and Pharisees mocked Jesus and challenged him to come down from the cross. The temptation to do this was of the same kind as that in the wilderness, namely, to compel belief by working a spectacular miracle. It was because he was saving others that he could not save himself.

The Synoptic Gospels and the Gospel of John record the following words spoken by Jesus from the cross:
1. 'Father, forgive them; they do not know what they are doing.' (Luke 23:34)
2. 'I tell you this: today you shall be with me in Paradise.' (Luke 23:43) (spoken to the dying criminal beside him)
3. 'Mother there is your son . . . There is your mother.' (John 19:26)
4. 'My God, my God, why hast thou forsaken me?' (Mark 15:34) (These are the most difficult of Jesus' words from the cross, since they imply that Jesus felt that God had abandoned him and that his trust had been misplaced. One explanation is that, since Jesus was bearing on the cross the sin of the whole world, he could not escape the consequences of that sin–an overwhelming sense of separation from God. The cry is a quotation from Psalm 22, a psalm which begins in despair but ends in triumph, and it is possible that Jesus had the whole psalm in mind.)
5. 'I thirst.' (John 19:28)

6. 'It is accomplished.' (John 19:30)
7. 'Father into thy hands I commit my spirit.' (Luke 23:46)

Jesus survived three hours on the cross and died at three o'clock. According to the Gospel records, darkness had covered the whole land during that period and, on the death of Jesus, the curtain of the Temple was torn in two. Matthew adds that after Jesus died there was an earthquake. The tearing of the Temple curtain (probably the one hanging over the entrance to the Holy of Holies) may be meant symbolically to represent the end of the old Jewish form of worship. Under that system, only the high priest had access to the Holy of Holies, where God dwelt, and that was only once a year. Through the death of Jesus, everyone–not just the high priest–had access to the presence of God. Whereas Matthew and Mark refer to the centurian's remarks suggesting that Jesus was one of the gods–'This was a son of God'–Luke's account states that Jesus was 'a righteous man'. Joseph of Arimathea was undoubtedly a man of some influence, otherwise his request to Pilate for the body of Jesus would have meant losing his position on the Jewish Council. According to Matthew's Gospel, the tomb was guarded on the instructions of Pilate, after a delegation of Pharisees and chief priests had warned him of the possibility of Jesus' disciples stealing the body (Matthew 27:62–66).

The Resurrection and Resurrection appearances

1. The empty tomb (Luke 24:1–12; Matthew 28:1–15; Mark 16:1–8)   The Gospels tell us that certain women went to the tomb on the Sunday morning with spices to anoint the body. They found that the stone at the entrance had been removed and the body was gone. Mark says that a young man (described by Matthew as an angel) in a white robe told them that Jesus had risen. In Luke's Gospel, the message is delivered by 'two men in dazzling garments'. The women concerned were Mary of Magdala, Joanna and Mary the mother of James, who reported what they saw to the apostles.

2. On the road to Emmaus (Luke 24:13–35)   Two of Jesus' disciples were on their way to a village called Emmaus, seven miles from Jerusalem. They were very sorrowful because of the death of their leader, and from their remark, 'we had been hoping that he was the man to liberate Israel', we may conclude that they still held the traditional view of the messiah. When Jesus approached them they did not recognize him, perhaps because they were so wrapped up in their grief. They talked together and Jesus explained that all that had happened was in fulfilment of the Law and the Prophets. Later, while Jesus was breaking the bread at a meal, he made himself known to them and then vanished from their sight. They returned to Jerusalem and told the other disciples.

3. The evening of Easter Day (Luke 24:36–43)   As the disciples from Emmaus were telling those in Jerusalem of their encounter with Jesus, he suddenly appeared in their midst. At first they were alarmed because they thought he was a spirit, but he reassured them by eating some boiled fish to prove that his body was as tangible as theirs.

4. A mountain in Galilee (Matthew 28:16–20)   Unlike the other appearances, which were in or near Jerusalem, this one took place in Galilee. The eleven disciples went to a mountain where Jesus had arranged to meet them. They were commissioned by him to convert all nations (Matthew 19 and 20).

The Ascension

Luke 24:50–53 tells us that Jesus led the disciples out to Bethany, and blessed them before leaving them. According to Mark's Gospel, Jesus was having a meal with the disciples and was then received up into heaven (Mark 16:19).

John in his Gospel records Jesus' appearance to Mary Magdalene (John 20:11–18), to the disciples in the upper room (John 20:19–23), and to Thomas (John 20:24–29).

Chapter 5
The Acts of the Apostles

The book in the New Testament entitled 'The Acts of the Apostles', provides the historical framework for the development of Christianity in the first century. We read there of the origin of the Christian Church in Jerusalem and how the faith spread throughout Judea and as far as Samaria, reaching then to Cyprus, Asia Minor and Greece. We read how the 'good news' of Jesus was preached to the Gentiles, thus spreading the word of God as revealed in the Gospels to the Jews.

It is generally believed that the book was written by Luke, to whom Paul referred as a 'fellow worker' (Philemon verse 24). Most scholars think that because the style of Luke's Gospel is similar to that of Acts and because they are both dedicated to a certain Theophilus, that they were written by the same person. It is thought that Acts was intended to be a sequel to the Gospel. There are a number of medical terms in both Luke's Gospel and Acts, and, since Luke was reputed to be a physician, this lends credence to the view that he was the author of both books. This does, however, remain a theory and we cannot be certain about it. The identity of Theophilus is also uncertain. He may have been a Roman official. It seems that at some stage on his travels Luke came into contact with Theophilus and was befriended by him.

One striking characteristic of Acts is its sympathy for the Gentile community in Palestine. This is clearly reflected in the author's inclusion of much material relating to the Gentiles. It is believed that the book was written in about AD 80.

The beginning of Acts records the Ascension of Jesus as taking place on the Mount of Olives forty days after the Resurrection (Acts 1:6–11). From this time onwards, **the disciples waited for the coming of the Holy Spirit as Jesus had promised**. They adopted the practice of meeting together in an upper room which may have been the same one as they had used for the Last Supper, at Mark's mother's house. **From the first, Peter assumed the leadership of the early Christian community in Jerusalem** and told them that they must choose another apostle to replace Judas (Acts 1:12–26). Two names were put forward for consideration, Joseph Barsabbas and Matthias. After prayer, the latter was chosen by lot. There may have been a wish in the Christian community to preserve some form of identity with the original twelve tribes of Israel by maintaining the number of apostles at twelve.

The Day of Pentecost (Acts 2)

Fifty days after the feast of Passover, the disciples were gathered together for the feast of Weeks, also known as Pentecost. On this occasion **the Holy Spirit came upon them and they could only describe the experience as like the rushing of a mighty wind**. They felt convinced that Jesus was with them and ran down into the street and **'began to talk in other tongues'**. At least they were so excited that that was how it seemed. One explanation often given for this is that the disciples spoke in Aramaic which everyone would understand, especially since there would have been Jews in Jerusalem from all countries of the Jewish dispersion. The apostles were accused of being drunk, a charge which Peter promptly denied since it was only nine in the morning.

Peter told the people gathered there that Old Testament prophecy was being fulfilled and that God was bestowing his spirit upon them as the prophet Joel had predicted:

> Thereafter the day shall come when I will pour out my spirit on all mankind; your sons and your daughters shall prophesy, your old men shall dream dreams and your young men see visions; I will pour out my spirit in those days even upon slaves and slave girls.

(Joel 2:28)

A new age had begun. Jesus had died but was now resurrected, as foretold in Psalm 16:8–11:

> I have set the Lord continually before me: with him at my right hand I cannot be shaken. Therefore my heart exults and my spirit rejoices, my body too rests unafraid; for thou

wilt not abandon me to Sheol nor suffer thy faithful servant to see the pit. Thou wilt show me the path of life; in thy presence is the fullness of joy, in thy right hand pleasures for evermore.

Jesus had ascended into heaven and had sent the Holy Spirit to guide his disciples. They were at this time overcome with excitement at the occurrence which was to motivate and strengthen them in their missionary work.

It is interesting to note that the facility for 'speaking with tongues' was said to be a common phenomenon in New Testament times. According to the apostle Paul it was quite common at Corinth. The word 'glossolalia', often used to describe the experience, was coined as late as the nineteenth century and so certainly does not go back to New Testament times or anything like it. The argument as to what exactly the experience involved still continues.

Assuming a position of authority, Peter told all those assembled to **repent and be baptized since all had sinned**. Three thousand people are said to have been baptized that day, now known as 'Whit-Sunday'. Baptism 'in the name of Jesus' was adopted as the initiation ceremony into Christianity.

The preaching and work of Peter (Acts 3 and 4)

Established as the leader of the community, Peter began preaching and healing with the apostle John. Once, when entering the Temple to pray (which, as Jews, they were entitled to do) **they met a man, a life-long cripple, who begged for alms. Peter commanded him in the name of Jesus to get up and walk, which he immediately did**, to the wonder and astonishment of the people. After this, the man went into the Temple with them.

Peter's speech outside the Temple (Acts 3:12–26), is similar to that made at Pentecost. Indeed, some scholars believe they may both be from a collection of speeches made by Peter on various occasions. Peter emphasized that it was really Jesus whom they had crucified who had healed the man. Jesus had risen from the dead and therefore they must all now repent of their evil deeds.

The Sadducees in particular were troubled by such references to the resurrection and the chief priests soon had them arrested for preaching about Jesus and brought them before the Sanhedrin. When given an opportunity to speak in defence of himself and John, Peter emphasized yet again that it was in the name of Jesus that they had healed the cripple. They were instructed not to teach about Jesus any more and then released, even though Peter announced they were duty bound to continue preaching.

Some time later, they were arrested again and on this occasion the rabbi **Gamaliel** (one of the teachers of the apostle Paul (Acts 22:3)) told the assembly to remember that **if the work of Peter and John was of God, it would succeed, but if it was the work of men, it would certainly perish**. The Sanhedrin took his advice, had the apostles beaten and again banned them from preaching about Jesus. It is probable that Gamaliel's advice saved the apostle's lives.

In his speech Gamaliel is reported as having referred to the rebellion of Theudas, though according to the Jewish historian Josephus, this did not take place until later, about AD 44–45. He also referred to the insurrection of Judas the Galilean who mounted a revolt in AD 6.

The early organization of the Church
The early Christians were expecting the second coming of Jesus soon and for this reason they prayed and worked together for the advancement of the faith, some having their property in common. The book of Acts records how Barnabas, a Greek Jew from Cyprus (of whom we hear more later in connection with Paul's missionary journeys) sold some of his land and gave the money to the Christian community. This was in contrast to Ananias and his wife Sapphira (Acts 5:1–12), who sold a property and brought only some of the proceeds to the apostles whilst pretending it was the whole sum. Peter told Ananias that he had lied to God, and, on hearing this, he dropped down dead. When his wife gave the same story she too died instantly. We might say they both suffered a heart attack from the shock of their deception being revealed to the apostles. In any event such practices as selling one's property and donating the money to the Christian community assumed less

importance as time passed and the apostles came to realize that Jesus' second coming would not be as soon as they had originally expected.

The seven deacons—Stephen the first Christian martyr (Acts 6–7)

Seven men were chosen to help with preaching and teaching (Acts 6:1–6), and in particular to care for the Hellenistic widows (widows of Jewish Christians outside Judea) as it was alleged that they were being neglected. These seven men were Jews of Greek descent who had become Christians and were said to be full of the Holy Spirit. They were chosen by the whole Christian community and then consecrated by the apostles through the laying on of hands. Their names were: Stephen, Philip, Prochorus, Nicanor, Timon, Parmenas and Nicolas of Antioch.

Stephen, one of the seven deacons, preached and worked miracles but was accused of blasphemy against God (Acts 6:8–7:60). He was arrested and brought before the Sanhedrin. In his defence Stephen spoke eloquently on the truth of Christianity. God, he said, had spoken to their ancestors before there was a Temple and before they even lived in Palestine. God's messengers, such as Joseph, Moses, the prophets and now especially Jesus, had been rejected, and now they were rejecting the Holy Spirit too:

> How stubborn you are, heathen still at heart and deaf to the truth! You always fight against the Holy Spirit. Like fathers, like sons. Was there ever a prophet whom your fathers did not persecute? They killed those who foretold the coming of the Righteous One; and now you have betrayed and murdered him, you who received the Law as God's angels gave it to you, and yet have not kept it.
>
> (Acts 7:51–53)

But it was the words that followed this that incensed those listening more than anything else, Luke tells us that Stephen, 'filled with the Holy Spirit, and gazing up to heaven, saw the glory of God, and Jesus standing at God's right hand. "Look," he said, "there is a rift in the sky; I can see the Son of Man standing at God's right hand!"' This was too much for the members of the Council. To them it was clear that Stephen was committing blasphemy to talk about God in this way. He must be stopped. Mob law then took over and he was taken out of the city and stoned. Death by stoning was the ritual penalty for blasphemy under Jewish Law (Leviticus 24:16). Acts mentions that a certain Saul of Tarsus watched the death of the first Christian martyr.

Philip preaches in Samaria (Acts 8:4–40)

When persecution by Saul became widespread in Jerusalem, Philip, another of the seven deacons, escaped to Samaria, where it is said that he preached and performed miracles. He met a magician called Simon Magus who was impressed by Philip and was baptized by him. In the Acts and in the New Testament as a whole we find a number of references to the appeal that magical arts held for the people of the time. Later, when Peter and John arrived there to lay their hands on those who had been baptized and had received the Holy Spirit, Simon offered them money in the hope of gaining the same power as they possessed. He was duly rebuked by Peter. Peter and John returned to Jerusalem, passing through Samaritan villages and preaching the Gospel as they went.

The Ethiopian eunuch

On his way to Gaza by the Mediterranean Sea, Philip met an Ethiopian eunuch, 'a high official of the Candace, or Queen of Ethiopia', who was probably an African and a Gentile. As such he would have been one of the God-fearers, that is, Gentiles who worshipped the one God of the Jews. He was returning from a pilgrimage to Jerusalem. This may have been the Feast of Tabernacles, since he was reading from one of the Servant Songs of the prophet Isaiah (Isaiah 53:7–8), which was a lesson related to that occasion. He was puzzled by what he read and so Philip explained to him that the Servant referred to in the passage was Jesus Christ. Following this explanation he asked Philip to baptize him. Philip continued on his way to Azotus, which was formerly known as Ashdod, and then went on to Joppa where he remained.

Paul's conversion (Acts 9:1–22)

There are three accounts of the conversion of Paul in the Acts: the passage mentioned above, Acts 22:6–11, and Acts 26:12–18.

Paul was born a member of the tribe of Benjamin, the son of a Roman citizen in Tarsus, a city in Cilicia, in Asia Minor. He was also a strict Pharisee. We learn later (Acts 18:3 and 20:34) that he earned his living by making tents.

In his zeal to defend the Jewish faith, Paul requested authority from the high priest at Jerusalem to arrest followers of the new 'way', who were regarded as heretics. On his way to Damascus to track down any Christians there, he saw a great light in the sky and heard the voice of Jesus who asked why he was persecuting him. Blinded by the light, he was led into Damascus, a hundred and fifty miles north east of Jerusalem. It has been suggested that he suffered from sunstroke as he may have been travelling at midday when the sun is very bright. The flash in the sky could also have been a lightning storm. He was taken to the house of a man called Judas who lived in Straight Street. A disciple called Ananias (not the Ananias referred to earlier) was told in a vision to meet Paul there. He laid his hands on Paul who received his sight back again. Paul was then baptized and became a follower of the faith, receiving the power of the Holy Spirit. When he began to preach about Jesus in the synagogue at Damascus, the Jews plotted against him and he had to escape with the aid of the Christians and headed for Jerusalem.

In Paul's letter to the Galatians, he refers to a visit to Arabia at this time (Galatians 1:7), which was probably to prepare quietly for his future work: ' . . . without consulting any human being, without going up to Jerusalem to see those who were apostles before me, I went off at once to Arabia, and afterwards returned to Damascus'. According to Galatians, it was three years after this that Paul went to Jerusalem 'to get to know' Peter, with whom he stayed for a fortnight. Though the Christians at Jerusalem were suspicious of Paul, he was welcomed by Barnabas, who was mentioned in Acts 4:36–37. In Jerusalem, too, the Jews plotted against him and he left for Caesarea and then Tarsus.

Peter as leader of the early Christian community (Acts 9:32–11:18)

As leader of the early Christian community, Peter began a preaching tour. He went first to Lydda, a village of Judea, where he healed Aeneas, a man who had been paralysed for eight years. He was asked if he would go to Joppa, eight miles away, to the house of Tabitha, who had died. He found her lying on her bed and restored her to life. These accounts of Peter's work are very similar to miracles found in the Gospels (Luke 5:18–26 and Mark 5:40).

While Peter was at Joppa he stayed at the house of Simon, a tanner. At this time **Cornelius**, a man who feared God and a centurian of the Italian Cohort, who lived at Caesarea, had a vision telling him to send for Peter at Joppa. Peter also had a vision when he was resting on the roof-top of the house. He dreamt he saw something like a sheet filled with 'unclean' animals, which descended from the sky three times and heard a voice telling him to kill and eat. As he was a Jew there were certain animals that his religion would have told him were unclean in the sense that they must not be eaten (Leviticus 11:1–32). He was told not to consider unclean anything which God had cleansed, and realized that no one was excluded from true contact with God simply because they were not Jewish.

When messengers arrived from Cornelius at Caesarea, Peter went with them to Cornelius' house and preached the news of the Christian faith to the family. The Holy Spirit came upon them and, seeing this, Peter baptized them. Peter learned that God would freely accept people who did not know or keep his Law as the Jews did. This is the **first account of Gentiles becoming Christians**.

When members of the church at Jerusalem heard of the conversion of Cornelius and his family, they questioned Peter carefully, particularly as he had stayed and eaten with them. When Peter told them about his vision and discussed the happenings at Caesarea with them, **they realized that Gentiles also were to receive the gospel of Jesus**.

Barnabas was sent by the church at Jerusalem to Antioch in Syria to inspect new developments there. He found Paul at Tarsus and took him to Antioch, where they worked together for a year. We are told at this point (Acts 11:26) that it was at Antioch that followers of Christ were first called Christians, which was initially

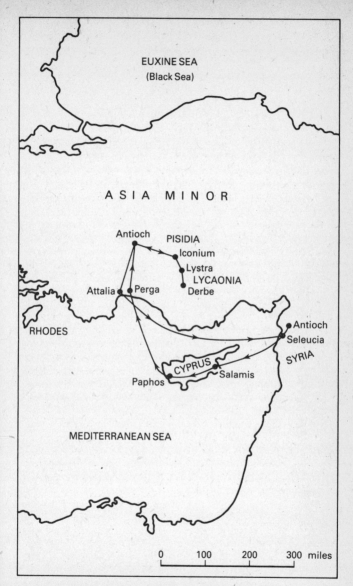

Figure 10. Paul's first missionary journey

a nickname. Agabus, a Christian prophet, foretold a famine in Judea (Acts 11:28), and contributions were sent by Barnabas and Paul to the elders at Jerusalem. This is the first reference to a Christian who is regarded as a prophet; it was a function which was of some importance in the very early days.

Difficult times were ahead for the Christians (Acts 12). Herod Agrippa I, grandson of Herod the Great, had James, the brother of John, beheaded. As this pleased the Jews, he proceeded to arrest Peter, who made a spectacular escape with the assistance of an 'angel'. A sympathetic admirer may have helped him elude the military guard. Agrippa died at Caesarea in AD 44, and was succeeded by his son, Herod Agrippa II.

Paul's first missionary journey (Acts 13–14)

Acts tells us that at Antioch Barnabas and Paul were commissioned by the laying on of hands to preach the word of God as sponsored missionaries. At that time (AD 46) Antioch became the great centre of the Christian faith. Filled with the Holy Spirit, they took with them John Mark, Barnabas' nephew, as their assistant, and sailed from the port of Seleucia, heading for **Cyprus**. They landed at the port of **Salamis**, the commercial centre of the island, where they preached in the synagogue. From there they proceeded to **Paphos**, the Roman capital, where Sergius Paulus, the Roman pro-consul lived. There they met Elymas, like Simon Magus, a magician, who was rebuked by Saul and struck blind temporarily for opposing them. From this point on, Saul's name appears as Paul (Acts 13:9), and Luke places Paul's name before that of Barnabas. Paul thus became the leader of the team when they set out for Asia Minor. On their arrival at **Perga**, John Mark left them for a reason unknown and returned to Jerusalem. We hear of him later in Paul's letters (Philemon verse 24; Colossians 4:10).

Paul preached his **first recorded sermon** at the Roman colony of **Antioch in Pisidia.** He told the assembly there that Jesus was the promised one, whom the Jews had rejected at Jerusalem. Paul was asked to speak again on the following Sabbath, when 'almost the whole city gathered to hear the word of God'. A hasty departure from the town was, however, forced upon him by Jewish opponents.

Paul and Barnabas went on to **Iconium**, where they preached in the synagogue but again had to escape when the Jews became jealous of the attention they were receiving from the people. We find at **Lystra** the **first record of a healing by Paul**, that of a cripple. The local people concluded that the apostles were gods, thinking Paul was Mercury (Greek Hermes), and Barnabas Jupiter (Greek Zeus). With some difficulty Paul convinced them that he and his companion were ordinary men and prevented them from offering a sacrifice to them. When Jews arrived from Antioch and Iconium in search of them, Paul was stoned by the mob and left for dead. Paul and Barnabas departed for Derbe, which was nearby. This was effectively the end of the outward journey. They then returned through Lystra, Iconium, and Antioch in Pisidia (where they appointed elders) and arrived back at Antioch in Syria. Their journey lasted some two years.

The question of Jew and Gentile: the Council of Jerusalem (Acts 15:1–33)

As it became clear that Gentiles were being admitted into the church, some members of the Christian community at Jerusalem went to Antioch and claimed that Gentiles should be circumcised when they accepted the faith. There developed two groups of Christians: those who had been strict Jews and those who had never had anything to do with the Jewish faith. It was agreed that Paul and Barnabas would go to Jerusalem to try to resolve the difficulty. There were possibly two meetings held there, one in private between the apostles and the elders when Paul and Barnabas gave a report about their missionary work, and one meeting in public. **Peter recommended tolerance towards the Gentiles and said that Jewish customs should not be imposed upon them**. Evidently acting as president of the meeting, James, known as 'the Just', summed up their conclusions: **Gentile converts were to abstain from: (i) the pollution of idols, (ii) fornication, (iii) things strangled, and (iv) blood. They were excused the rite of circumcision**. A letter giving details of the agreement reached at Jerusalem was sent to the church at Antioch via Judas Barsabbas and Silas, together with Paul and Barnabas.

95

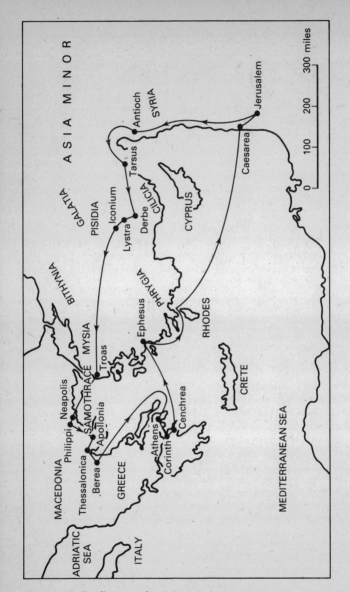

Figure 11. Paul's second missionary journey

The Acts of the Apostles does not tell us anything about Peter after the Council. Legend has it that he was crucified at Rome head downwards, not considering himself worthy of the same manner of death as Jesus.

Paul's second missionary journey (Acts 15:36–18:22)

It was Paul's wish to revisit the places where he had preached on the first missionary journey, but, before they set off, there was a difference of opinion between Paul and Barnabas over John Mark whom Barnabas wanted to take with them. Paul objected to this because John Mark had left them at Perga at the beginning of the first missionary journey. The two apostles therefore parted company. Barnabas left for Cyprus with John Mark, while Paul took Silas with him through Syria and Cilicia to the places he had visited with Barnabas. Paul and Silas travelled to **Derbe**, and then to **Lystra**, where Paul met a disciple called Timothy, whom he wished to accompany him on his journey and whom he had circumcised. This would seem to be at variance with Paul's views but was probably explained by Timothy's half-Jewish parenthood. They then travelled across to **Troas**, where they may have been joined by Luke, as the 'we' passages in Acts now commence, suggesting that these were exact words from a diary and that Luke was the author. The 'we' passages in Acts are as follows:

1. Acts 16:9–18, from Troas to Philippi;
2. Acts 20:4–16, from Philippi to Miletus;
3. Acts 21:1–18, from Miletus to Jerusalem;
4. Acts 27:1–28:16, from Caesarea to Rome.

At Troas Paul had a vision of a man calling him to come over to Macedonia. They sailed from Troas to an island called Samothrace, and from there to Neapolis, the port of Philippi, where they disembarked and made for **Philippi**. This was a Roman colony and was named after Philip of Macedon, the father of Alexander the Great. As there was no synagogue there, Paul preached by the river and Lydia, a dealer in dye, was converted, together with her household. Paul and Silas met a slave girl who was considered to have psychic powers which her owners exploited as a source of income. Believing she was possessed, Paul commanded the demon to come out of her in the name of Jesus.

When her masters saw that they had lost their profit from her, they had Paul and Silas arrested, beaten and imprisoned. During the night there was an earthquake–a common occurrence in that part of Macedonia–which rocked the prison and freed the prisoners from their cells. Fearing that the prisoners had escaped, the jailor was about to kill himself, but Paul reassured him, and, at his request, preached the gospel to him. The event ended happily with the conversion of the jailor and the baptism of his whole family. When the magistrates ordered their release, Paul pointed out that they were Roman citizens and their imprisonment had been unlawful. The magistrates came and apologized and asked them to leave the city.

The apostles then travelled via Amphipolis and Apollonia to **Thessalonica**, a city known today as Salonika. In Paul's day it was the capital of the Roman province of Macedonia. Paul preached in the synagogue there on three sabbaths. The Jews became jealous of Paul and attacked the house of Jason where he and Silas were staying. They arrested Jason but could not find Paul and Silas who left by night for **Berea**. Here they were welcomed at the synagogue and close attention was paid to their message but trouble arose with the arrival of Jews from Thessalonica, and Paul continued to Athens, leaving Silas and Timothy behind to rejoin him later.

At **Athens** Paul was invited by the Epicureans and the Stoics to explain the new religion he preached. They took him to the Court of Areopagus, where the highest judicial court sat and here he gave an account of his beliefs. In his address, Paul referred to the particularly religious nature of the people of Athens. He mentioned that, among all the altars in their city, he had seen one dedicated to an unknown God, whom they worshipped in ignorance. He could now tell them about this God. He was the creator of all things and existed before the creation of the world. This God did not need temples or sacrifices. He was in control of all things and everything came under his jurisdiction. Men, as his creation, needed God and should repent of their sins since he had decreed that they would one day all be judged by Jesus Christ who had risen from the dead (Acts 17:22–31). When Paul spoke of Jesus and the resurrection they laughed and said they would hear more later, but he did convert Dionysius, a member of the Council and some others, including a woman called Damaris.

Epicurus, who lived about 300 BC, was the founder of the **Epicureans**, and he maintained that happiness should be one's goal in life, though he stressed the importance of moderation in all things. He claimed that all truth could be found in the senses. Followers of this school of thought therefore did not believe in immortality.

The **Stoics** were so called after the word 'stoa', or porch in Athens, where, in about 300 BC, Zeno of Citium taught that God created and maintained the world. He affirmed man's moral values and suggested people should accept their fate and live by their reasoning.

Paul left Athens for **Corinth**, which at that time had a bad reputation for its immorality. He stayed with Aquila and Priscilla who were, like Paul, tentmakers, or possibly workers in leather. Silas and Timothy rejoined him and 'sabbath by sabbath' he taught in the synagogue there. When trouble arose again with the Jews, Paul said he would take his message to the Gentiles and stayed for eighteen months with Titius Justus, who, in fact, lived next to the synagogue. A charge brought by the Jews against Paul was summarily dismissed by Gallio, the proconsul of Achaia. Accompanied by Aquila and Priscilla, Paul then left for Cenchrea, where he took a boat to Ephesus, the capital of the Roman province of Asia, where Aquila and Priscilla remained while Paul went on to Caesarea and from there to Jerusalem.

The third missionary journey (Acts 18:23–21:26)

After a short while, Paul set out on a third missionary journey. While he passed through Galatia and Phrygia, Apollos, an Alexandrian Jew, arrived at Ephesus and began teaching in the synagogue. He had received only the baptism of John and was taught further by Aquila and Priscilla, and then sent on to Corinth. Paul arrived at **Ephesus** after Apollos had left. He met and baptized twelve men who also only knew John's baptism. He preached first to the Jews in the synagogue for three months and

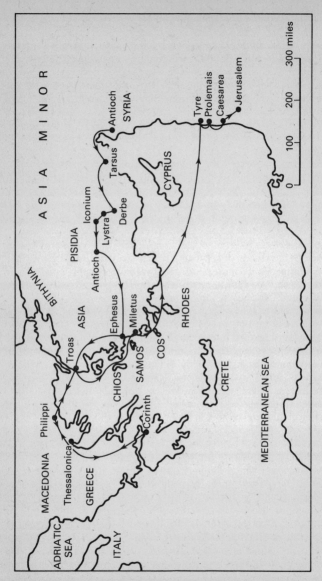

Figure 12. Paul's third missionary journey

then to the Gentiles at the lecture theatre of the philosopher, Tyrannus for two years. During this time, he performed many healings and exorcisms. The seven sons of Sceva, a Jewish priest, attempted to copy Paul in his work with disastrous results for themselves. Many people who used to practise magic were converted by Paul and publicly burned their books of magic.

Ephesus was the seat of the great temple to Diana, one of the seven ancient wonders of the world. Paul's teaching against idolatry so diminished the profits of the silversmiths who made statuettes of Diana for their living, that, led on by one Demetrius, they staged a huge riot in the town which was only suppressed after the local 'town clerk' had threatened them with the displeasure of the Roman authorities. As far as Paul was concerned, this was a clear example of the truth being attacked by vested interests dressed up as religion.

After leaving Ephesus, Paul went to **Macedonia**, where he greeted the Christians. He stayed in Greece for three months. At **Philippi** he met Luke again (Acts 20:6), and together they continued to **Troas**. We find, in fact, that the 'we' passages take us as far as Miletus. At Troas they joined in the breaking of bread on Sunday and stayed seven days. It was at Troas also that Eutychus fell from a window while listening to Paul preach late at night and was restored to life by him. At Assos Paul took a boat for Mitylene and sailed from there to Chios and Samos. When he arrived at the port of **Miletus** Paul asked the elders from Ephesus to meet him. He addressed them in loving terms and then made his farewell. He then continued via Cos and Rhodes to Patara, where he changed ship for Tyre, and spent seven days there. After a night at Ptolemais, he arrived at **Caesarea**, where he stayed several days with Philip. At Caesarea he also met Agabus, the prophet mentioned in Acts 11:28, who foretold Paul's imprisonment at Jerusalem. Despite the entreaties of the Christians at Caesarea, Paul was determined to continue his journey to Jerusalem.

Paul at Jerusalem (Acts 21:17 – 23:35)
At Jerusalem, Paul met leaders of the church who expressed their pleasure at the work that he had done. Reference was made,

however, to a report that he had advocated to some Christians the abandoning of Jewish practices. To counteract such rumours they suggested that Paul underwent a Nazarite vow for a short period, together with four other men whose expenses for the vow he was to pay, thereby showing that he kept the holy law.

One day when Paul was in the Temple during the period of his vow, certain Asian Jews accused him of teachings against the Jewish religion. They also claimed that he had taken a Gentile, called Trophimus (one of the seven companions of Paul referred to in Acts 20:4) into the Temple, the penalty for which was death. As they were dragging him out of the Temple to kill him, Paul was rescued by the Roman captain of the guard from the nearby Castle of Antonia, to whom he spoke in Greek. He was given the opportunity to address the crowd, which he did in Aramaic. In his defence, he emphasized his Jewish background and reminded them how he used to persecute the Christians and was then himself converted. When he spoke of preaching to the Gentiles, the crowd shouted at him and became very agitated. At this point, the captain ordered him to be taken into the barracks and was about to have him flogged when Paul protested that he was a Roman citizen. Roman law forbad the flogging of its own citizens.

The following day, the captain brought Paul before the Sanhedrin. It is not certain why he did this, or whether it was a formal or informal meeting. Paul divided the Pharisees and the Sadducees at the meeting and created an uproar by saying that he was a Pharisee and that his only offence was his belief in a resurrection. He was then returned to prison. Acts tells us how Paul's nephew warned the captain of the guard of a Jewish plot to kill Paul (Acts 23:16). This is the only reference in Acts to Paul's family. Paul was subsequently taken by night to Caesarea and later brought before the governor Felix.

Paul before the Roman governors (Acts 24–26)
In the trial before **Felix**, Tertullus, a professional lawyer, spoke on behalf of Ananias, the high-priest, and the other Jews who had arrived from Jerusalem. He accused Paul of: (a) being a nuisance, (b) rebelling against Rome, (c) being leader of the sect known as

the Nazarenes, and (d) profaning the Temple. Paul objected to the accusations and maintained that he had gone to Jerusalem to worship the God of the Jews and had not profaned the Temple, though he admitted to being a member of the new 'way'. Felix deferred the trial and put Paul under open arrest, thus allowing him to receive visitors. The book of Acts suggests that Felix was expecting a bribe from Paul to free him.

Two years later, Felix was succeeded by **Porcius Festus** who was a governor from AD 58–61, and Paul was summoned to appear before him. It was at this time that Paul made his famous **appeal to go before Caesar** (Acts 25:11–12), as was his right as a Roman citizen. At the suggestion of Festus, Paul appeared before **King Agrippa II** when he came to Caesarea, though this may not have been a formal trial. Paul defended himself before Agrippa as he had done before the crowd at Jerusalem by referring to the way in which he used to persecute the followers of Jesus, and how he too became a follower of the faith. In his reply to Paul, Agrippa was somewhat cynical but still courteous and used the word 'Christian', perhaps as a nickname. This is only the second use of the word in Acts. The first reference we saw in Acts 11:26. We find the word also used in 1 Peter 4:16. Agrippa and Festus both felt Paul was not guilty of any crime.

The journey to Rome (Acts 27–28)

Paul began his journey to Rome under the direction of a centurian called Julius. At Caesarea they boarded a ship whose home port was Adramyttium. At Sidon Paul was allowed to visit friends, and then they proceeded to Myra, where they changed ships and headed for Cnidus and then Fair Havens, a harbour of Crete, where Paul suggested that, in view of the bad weather, they should spend the winter. It was decided to continue, but the incident does demonstrate that Paul was evidently held in high regard for them even to listen to his suggestion. They passed an island called Cauda and approached the coast of Africa, where they ran into trouble and were shipwrecked on the island of Malta. Here they were well received by the inhabitants and, indeed, when Paul was bitten by a venomous snake and suffered no harm, they believed him to be a god. For three days Paul was entertained by Publius, the chief magistrate. The company stayed on the island for three months in all, after which they set sail for Rome in a ship called the *Castor and Pollux*. They travelled via Syracuse, Rhegium and Puteoli, and finally arrived at The Three Taverns and Rome, where Paul stayed for some two years at lodgings at his own expense, welcoming all who came to visit him.

According to tradition, Paul was acquitted at his trial and resumed his missionary journeys to Asia Minor and perhaps to Spain. He is believed to have been arrested on a further occasion and sent again to Rome, where finally, about AD 65, under the persecution of the Emperor Nero, he was executed by beheading.

Chapter 6
The Letters of Paul

The letters of Paul are the earliest New Testament writings we have and, while it is difficult to be precise about dates, they were probably written between AD 50 and AD 58. We cannot be certain which letters were in fact written by Paul himself, even when they are attributed to him, nor can we be sure about the order in which they were written. The following are traditionally believed to be written by the apostle:

1 Thessalonians	Philemon
2 Thessalonians	Ephesians
1 Corinthians	Philippians
2 Corinthians	1 Timothy
Galatians	2 Timothy
Romans	Titus
Colossians	

Some of these letters were sent to churches that Paul had founded. Examples of these are: 1 and 2 Thessalonians, 1 and 2 Corinthians, Galatians, and probably Philippians. Others, such as the letters to the Romans, and Colossians, were written to churches founded by his converts or other Christian leaders. Some of his letters, such as those to Timothy and Titus, known as the Pastoral Epistles, were addressed to individuals, as was the letter to Philemon.

Paul's letters cover a variety of topics and provide details of his life which supplement in many ways those given in the Acts of the Apostles, reflecting the atmosphere in an early Christian community. They give details about Paul's teaching to the Christian community and the kind of problems he encountered. It must be remembered that he wrote for specific communities and their particular problems, rather than for the whole church.

1 and 2 Thessalonians
These letters were probably written from Corinth while Paul was there for some eighteen months, perhaps during AD 50/51 on his

second missionary journey, some time after leaving Thessalonica. His assistant, Timothy, had brought news of the progress of the Christians at Thessalonica and this prompted Paul to write the first letter to the church there. The letters describe the situation prevailing in an early Christian community whose members clearly expected an early return of Jesus. In view of the similarity in content of 1 and 2 Thessalonians, it has been suggested by some scholars that the first letter was written to pagan converts in Thessalonica and the second to Jewish Christians there. One reason for this suggestion is that 2 Thessalonians, as opposed to 1 Thessalonians, contains many references to the Old Testament.

1 Thessalonians

Paul began his first letter to the Thessalonians by sending them his greetings and commending them for their faith (1 Thessalonians 2:13–14). They had proved themselves to be an example to the other churches in the provinces of Macedonia and Achaia (1 Thessalonians 1:7, 8). They had been steadfast in their faith in spite of persecution by the Jews whom God, he said, would condemn. Their persistence in the faith doubtless pleased Paul, bearing in mind his marked lack of success at Athens. They were now following the true and living God, rather than worshipping idols.

Paul referred to certain accusations that had been levelled against him. Certain people had suggested that he attempted to gain popularity and he refuted this allegation strongly. He also emphasized that he had always earned his own living and urged them to do the same (I Thessalonians 4:11). They were to avoid any form of immorality but should love and help their fellow Christians. He stressed above all else the importance of brotherly love (I Thessalonians 4:9).

Some members of the church were worried about the position of those who had already died before the second coming of Jesus, which they expected soon. Paul told them not to concern themselves about these Christians since, at the resurrection, they would rise first and then all would be raised with Jesus together. **There was no doubt in the minds of the Christians of Thessalonica that Jesus**

106

would come again. **Indeed, Paul evidently expected this to take place in his life-time (I Thessalonians 4:15)**. He was concerned that they should not be over-eager in expecting the time when they would all be 'caught up in the clouds to meet the Lord in the air' (1 Thessalonians 4:17). He said that this day would come suddenly–'like a thief in the night'.

2 Thessalonians

This letter could be considered as a modification of Paul's first letter to the church at Thessalonica, though it is more formal in approach. He began with similar greetings to church members and told them that he was proud of the way they were keeping the faith, even in the face of increased persecution from the Jews.

Paul corrected certain false ideas about the second coming of Jesus. **It seems that some members of the church were inclined to think that they need not work any more, believing that the end of the present world was near at hand.** Paul reminded them that he himself had worked while he was with them and had not been an expense to anyone (2 Thessalonians 3:6–12). He pointed out that certain events were to take place before the end of the world took place, and they should be patient and prepare for the Day in the right manner. They were to take no notice of those who said that the Day had already arrived because the Anti-Christ, the embodiment of wickedness, had yet to come. He would reveal many false signs and wonders and eventually be destroyed. There was at this time a popular belief among people in the East that at the end of the world there would be a great battle between God and the forces of evil. Paul urged the Christians to remain faithful to the teaching they had received from him, whatever false prophets might say. When the expected return of Jesus did not take place, the early Christians had to modify their views.

1 and 2 Corinthians

We have already noted when dealing with Paul's second missionary journey, that Corinth, one of the largest cities in the Roman Empire, with a population of some five thousand people, was notorious for its immorality. This immorality was largely due to the worship of the Greek goddess Aphrodite, at whose shrine one thousand sacred prostitutes served.

It is generally thought that Paul wrote at least four letters to the Christians at Corinth. He may have written as many as six letters, of which we have now only fragments. The following scheme of events regarding Paul's writing is generally accepted:
1. Paul's first letter to the Corinthians. This is now lost or perhaps some of it is contained in 2 Corinthians 6:14–7:1. This, it is thought, dealt with the relationship between Christian leaders and pagans.
2. The second letter might have been the existing 1 Corinthians.
3. The third letter is thought to be chapters 10–13 of 2 Corinthians. This has been called the 'Severe letter', though these chapters may be only a part of the original letter.
4. The fourth letter of Paul to the Corinthians is believed to be 2 Corinthians 1–9, called the 'Thankful letter', since by the time Paul wrote this letter the situation in Corinth had much improved.

1 Corinthians

1 Corinthians was probably written from Ephesus during the third missionary journey, about AD 55. Paul visited Corinth after Athens on his second missionary journey and stayed there for eighteen months (Acts 18:1). He also stayed in Corinth on his third missionary journey (Acts 20:3), and may have visited it on other occasions too. After his visits he wrote this letter with very specific problems in mind. He had heard disturbing news about the situation of the church in Corinth. Paul had three sources of information: he had heard from Christians who used to meet at the house of Chloe (1 Corinthians 1:11), and may have been slaves there; from the Corinthians, Stephanas, Fortunatus, and Achaicus, who had visited him (1 Corinthians 16:17), and he had also received a letter which they had brought to him written by the Corinthian Christians (1 Corinthians 7:1).

After greeting members of the church at Corinth, **Paul expressed concern in his letter about the cliques or divisions that were forming among them**. One group apparently supported Paul, another Apollos, a third group supported Peter (which suggests that it was the more

Jewish party) and yet another group said they were adherents of Christ. Paul emphasized the unity of the body of Christ. The church was God's temple and Christ was the only foundation. For this reason, no one leader of the church should receive more importance than another.

Immorality was also a problem among members of the church. There had evidently been a case of incest in the Christian community—a man had been living with his father's wife. Paul declared that the person concerned was to be excommunicated from the church immediately. One's body, said Paul, was to be treated with respect because it belonged to Christ. Sexual intercourse should signify more than the satisfaction of one's physical needs.

Paul was also concerned about the **increasing practice of Christians going to 'heathen' courts for what were really small matters** (1 Corinthians 6:1–11), and urged them to settle such disputes between themselves with the help of their fellow-Christians.

Concerning **marital relationships**, Paul recommended church members not to marry, though it was certainly permitted as a 'second best' course of action. This was because he fully expected the world to end fairly soon and a new life to begin. **Divorce** for Christians was not commended, though 1 Corinthians 7:15 expressly accepts divorce for the Christian if it is demanded by the pagan partner. The Christian has no reason to feel guilty in such a case. **Widows** were allowed to remarry if the man they wished to marry was a Christian, but widowhood, he said was better. In these considerations Paul made no distinction between Jew and Gentile, freeman or slave.

Regarding **food which had been offered to idols**, Paul said that one's main aim was not to cause offence to anyone over eating this meat. Christians must act out of consideration for others. They must respect the feelings and scruples of others. In any event, they must not attend heathen sacrificial feasts.

Paul was concerned about what should be **the Christian attitude to living and worship**. Some Christians were not treating the Lord's

Supper in the right manner. It seems that when the Christians at Corinth met for worship, they divided themselves into groups instead of forming one community. Furthermore, each one was intent on eating his own food with no regard for anyone who was going hungry. They were all looking upon the occasion as an opportunity for a feast. Such an approach to the Lord's Supper Paul roundly condemned. Paul recalled the words of Jesus on his last evening before he was crucified and warned his readers of eating the bread and drinking the cup of the Lord unworthily. If they did so they were guilty of 'desecrating' the body and blood of the Lord. Paul's advice to the people, therefore, was to eat at home if they were hungry and so not abuse the Lord's Supper. It was a question of adopting the right attitude towards their worship. They had one Lord, one God. It was right that they should worship him together. They were, after all, brought into one body through baptism and 'one Holy Spirit was poured out for all of us to drink' (1 Corinthians 12:13).

Women, said Paul, should be veiled and have their heads covered at worship. In every respect they should be suitably attired (1 Corinthians 11:2–16). Indeed, all worship was to be conducted with dignity. Paul's readers were also to remember that all spiritual gifts were to be used for the benefit of the whole community. The greatest of these gifts was love.

Some Christians had doubted that there was a resurrection of the body after death. Paul assured them, in what is the earliest detailed account of the resurrection appearances, that Jesus Christ had indeed risen. He was victorious over death. By his resurrection, he had guaranteed that Christians would rise from the dead and enter the next life. They would all then have 'spiritual' bodies, rather than 'material' bodies. Paul concluded the letter by sending his greetings to the church at Corinth and recommending they gave what they could in the way of free-will offerings for those in need at Jerusalem.

2 Corinthians

In his second letter to the church at Corinth Paul was at pains to **defend his work and his authority**. He had been accused of insincerity and of failing to make a visit to Corinth. Both charges he refuted. He was relieved to hear that there had been a change of heart and attitude on their part about accusations made against him. He need worry no more about them. Paul urged the Christians at Corinth to give freely for the church at Jerusalem. They were to be like Jesus Christ who became poor for the sake of others, that they in turn might become spiritually rich. The last section of the letter, i.e. chapters 10–13, have already been referred to as the 'Severe letter'. It is so called because it contains a number of rebukes for its recipients as they had questioned his authority and apostolic status which he defended with great force.

Galatians

Galatians is a passionate letter about Christian freedom and was probably written after Paul's first missionary journey when he visited Antioch in Pisidia, Iconium, Lystra and Derbe (Acts 14 and 16), (i.e. the people in South Galatia whom he revisited on his second missionary journey). It may have been written before the 'Council' at Jerusalem (Acts 15). Certainly Paul makes no reference in his letter to the findings of the Council and it is thought by some scholars to be the first of Paul's letters. Many scholars now believe, however, that it was written some years later and was addressed to the people of North Galatia, whom Paul may have visited on his second and third missionary journeys (Acts 16:6 and 18:23).

The letter can be neatly divided into three sections: chapters 1 and 2 which are personal and apologetic in nature (i.e. they make a reasoned defence of Paul's position and of the Christian faith), chapters 3, 4 and 5, which are doctrinal, and chapter 6, which is of a practical nature. **The letter is particularly concerned with the question of whether the church should remain Jewish or spread outwards and include Gentiles.**

Paul's greeting to the people could aptly be described as lukewarm. He rebuked the Christian community for being drawn away from the faith by false teachers. These people also disputed Paul's apostolic authority and maintained that Christians should not forsake the Jewish faith and the rite of circumcision. Paul therefore defended his position. The Galatian Christians were foolish, he said, for they should not take any notice of those who undermined his work by claiming that the gospel he preached was not complete and that they needed to be circumcised. Paul had, in fact, heard that some of the Christians had been circumcised and he considered this was a retrograde step to have taken.

In defence of his apostolic authority, Paul told them that he had received his message from Christ and not from men. He had not spoken to the other apostles about his work until some years after his conversion. He had worked on his own in Syria and Cilicia and considered himself on an equal footing with the other apostles. Indeed, on one occasion at Antioch he had even taken Peter to task over the Jewish-Gentile question: 'I opposed him to his face because he was clearly in the wrong' (Galatians 2:11). (Peter had been quite happy to eat with Gentiles, but, under pressure from his Jewish colleagues, he ceased to do so. Paul condemned his hypocrisy.)

Paul emphasized **the importance of faith**. For him, faith meant saying 'yes' to all that God has done for men in and through Christ, and letting it control one's life. He said that salvation was given free by means of faith. It could not be obtained by observing the Law: because no one could keep the Law perfectly, all stood condemned by it. It was by faith rather than by following the Law that people gained God's blessing. There was thus a new relationship with God. Jew and Gentile were now equal. The Gentiles who had faith were considered to be the true heirs of the promise of God. The Jewish Law was only a temporary measure, the 'tutor' to bring men to Christ (Galatians 3:24). Paul emphasized that Abraham had put his faith in God and that faith had counted as righteousness.

The responsibility of the Christian, Paul pointed out, was to live by the Spirit. Christians were to bear one another's burdens and work for the benefit of the whole Church. They were no longer required to follow Jewish ritual requirements but that did not mean that they were free to do as they pleased. They were to live like Christ, filling their lives with good works and remembering that the 'harvest' of the Spirit is 'love, joy, peace, patience, kindness, goodness, fidelity, gentleness and self-control' (Galatians 5:22).

Romans

Paul's letter to the Romans–generally considered his greatest–was probably written from Corinth in about AD 56, while he was on his third missionary journey and before he set out on his return journey to Jerusalem. It was written to Christians whom he had not yet met, and in it he prepared the way for his intended visit to the Roman capital (Acts 19:21), which he hoped to use as a base. The church there probably consisted of mainly Gentile Christians (Romans 1:13) but it is possible that it also contained a strong Jewish element.

The letter is the most systematic account of Paul's thinking and teaching. Some of it is presented as spoken by an imaginary opponent who asks questions about the Christian faith in order that Paul can answer them. There are four principal sections to the letter:
1. the problem of man's relationship with God (chapters 1–8);
2. the rejection of the Messiah by the Jews (chapters 9–11);
3. Christian behaviour (chapters 12–15:13);
4. personal greetings (chapters 15:14–16:27).

1. The problem of man's relationship with God (chapters 1–8) After greeting the Christians at Rome and expressing a thanksgiving for their faith, Paul emphasized to his readers that Christianity was a universal religion and could be received by anyone. God demanded perfect holiness and however hard people might try to achieve this, it was obviously unattainable. People could not be saved by trying to keep the Jewish Law or by rituals such as circumcision. Salvation was a gift from God which was received through faith in Christ (Romans 4:5).

Reiterating what is now a familiar theme of his, Paul pointed out that the Jews had not kept the Law and were not in a better position than the Gentiles. They were not specially favoured by God since God has no favourites (Romans 2:11). Jew and Gentile alike had failed to meet God's standards. They were equal before God and would be treated as such. Paul said that the patriarch Abraham (who was much revered by the Jews) was accepted by God not because of his goodness but because of his faith in God (Romans 4:3). The faith of the Christians was to form the basis for the new relationship with God. Christ had died on behalf of sinners, taking on himself the punishment due to them. Those who put their faith in him were accepted by God, their sins were forgiven and they received eternal life: their sinful nature had died and the 'new man' had been born. They were under the power of God rather than that of sin. They were guided by the Spirit and were no longer burdened by the Jewish Law with all its requirements and restrictions but rather lived according to the law of faith. Nothing could now separate them from the love of God (Romans 8:28–39).

2. The rejection of the messiah by the Jews (chapters 9–11) Paul said that because the Jews did not have faith in Jesus Christ they had, in effect, brought about the preaching of Christianity to the Gentiles. He pointed out, however, that God had not completely rejected the Jews, his people, as eventually they would be included with the whole of the Christian community. God would show mercy to everyone.

3. Christian behaviour (chapters 12–15:13) This section deals with a number of ethical matters relating to the Christian way of life. The obligations of the Christian are set out, demonstrating how Christians must dedicate themselves to God (Romans 12:1–3), and show brotherliness, charity and forgiveness to others. They must show clearly that they care about other people. They must respect the State and its officials (Romans 13:1–7), remembering that all authority comes from God. Their behaviour must be correct, bearing in mind the closeness of the Last Day (Romans 13:11–14). All of their actions were to be guided by the law of love.

4. Personal greetings (chapters 15:14–16:27) This section is different from the rest of the letter in so far as a number of greetings are included which are addressed to individual people. We find here a letter of introduction for Phoebe who belonged to the church at Cenchrea, the eastern port of Corinth. Phoebe probably delivered the letter to the church at Rome. It is believed by some that chapter 15 did not form part of the original letter and certain scholars maintain that chapter 16 was written to another church, perhaps at Ephesus, where Paul had many friends and this would explain the presence of the personal references.

114

Colossians

It is generally believed that, like the letters to Philemon, the Ephesians and the Philippians, the letter to the Colossians was written by Paul from prison (Colossians 4:3,10). These are called 'Captivity Letters'. An imprisonment at Rome, Caesarea or Ephesus itself has been suggested. The letter is addressed to a church at Colossae, a city in the valley of the Lycus, at that time in the province of Asia. There is no record in Acts of a visit by Paul to Colossae (Colossians 2:1). It is possible that Paul had learned of the church there from a certain Epaphras, or Epaphroditus, (not the Christian referred to in Philippians 2:25), who may have been its founder. It seems that the church at Colossae was composed mainly of Gentile Christians.

Paul began by sending a greeting to the church at Colossae and expressing thanks for its spiritual growth and the increase in membership. He then referred to certain errors threatening the church: **false teachers were claiming that it was not enough to have faith in Christ in order to gain salvation**. They were saying that Christians should follow the Jewish Law and **practise circumcision** (Colossians 2:11); **observe feast days** (Colossians 2:16); **avoid unclean food** (Colossians 2:21); **worship angels** (Colossians 2:18) and **keep ascetic practices** (Colosssians 2:23). They should, it was said, also **follow a secret wisdom** (Colossians 2:2–3). These teachings were based on the doctrine that all matter was evil and that one needed the angels as mediators to approach God. The teachers were apparently trying to graft onto Christianity rites and beliefs which some Jews had adopted from Hellenistic thought.

Paul, in his reply, emphasized that true knowledge comes from God and that Christ is the only mediator between people and God. He insisted that Christ was superior to all other beings. Christians were to follow the new life in the Spirit rather than follow ascetic practices. Christ's death on the cross on their behalf had freed them from the restraints of the Law. They were to take no notice of those who told them what to eat and drink.

Paul reminded the Colossians of the demands of Christian conduct, which he saw as an essential part of the Christian faith. They were to be humble, gentle, loving and forgiving. At this point, Paul gave his readers guidance about correct relationships between husbands and wives, parents and children, and masters and slaves. They should demonstrate a caring and respectful attitude towards one another, remembering that everything should be done 'in the name of the Lord Jesus, giving thanks to God the Father through him' (Colossians 3:17).

Philemon

Paul's epistle to Philemon is a private letter to a man of Colossae whom Paul had evidently converted to Christianity and who was, at this time, an important member of the church. It seems that his house was large enough for Christians to hold meetings there. This letter was probably delivered at the same time as the letter to the Colossians. **It concerns a certain Onesimus, a slave who had run away** from Philemon, and who had approached Paul while he was in prison and become a Christian. Paul was now sending him back to Philemon with the plea that he would pardon him and treat him as a fellow Christian (verse 16). It is a tactful letter, containing no suggestion that Philemon should release Onesimus and no argument about the propriety of slavery. The punishment at this time for slaves deserting their masters could be crucifixion or torture. Since the letter was included with Paul's other letters in the New Testament, it would appear that Philemon must have forgiven Onesimus.

Ephesians

The letter to the Ephesians is somewhat similar in content to the letter to the Colossians. The author is dealing with similar problems. There are, however, none of the usual greetings to friends at the beginning of the letter. This is all the more surprising since, according to Acts 19, Paul spent quite a long time at Ephesus—possibly more than two years, and according to Acts 20:17–38, he met the leaders of the church of Ephesus at Miletus. It seems to be a letter sent to a church that Paul had not founded and whose members he did not know (Ephesians 1:15;3:2). It is therefore possible that Paul may not be the author. It has been suggested that the letter was a circular sent to the churches in Asia, and this suggestion is supported by the fact that early manuscripts do not include the words 'in Ephesus' in the greeting. The style, language and teaching are not typical of Paul, but the difficulties by no means rule out the possibility of Pauline authorship.

There are two parts to the letter, a theological part (Ephesians 1:1–3:21), where Paul gave thanks for Christ and the Christian faith, and a practical part (Ephesians 4:1–6:24), where he instructed his readers about the duties of a Christian within the family.

1. Giving thanks for Christ and the Christian Church (Ephesians 1:1–3:21) Paul reminded his readers that they had been saved by faith in Christ rather than by works of the Law. God had made Christ head of the church and Paul looked forward to the growth and development of the church throughout the world. Through Christ, all the former barriers and hostilities were broken down, and because of their mutual faith in him, Jews and Gentiles could have fellowship with each other. Everyone, said Paul, is on an equal footing in God's family. The church was the true temple.

2. The family (Ephesians 4:1–6:24) Paul set out the duties of members of the church and how these should affect their daily lives. They were to set an example to others in how they behaved. The church consisted of individuals bound together by their faith to form a united body. They all had separate roles to play in the church and they each had their own special gifts to bring to its well-being (Ephesians 4:7–16).

Paul contrasted their former life with the life that they had now adopted and listed the virtues necessary for members of the church. They should show the same kind of love as Christ did and imitate him (Ephesians 4:25–5:2), exhibiting such qualities as self-control and truthfulness. They should avoid dishonesty, indecency and ill-temper. As directed in Colossians, wives were to obey their husbands, husbands were to love their wives, and children were to obey their parents. Parents, in turn, were urged to treat their children with understanding. As in other Pauline correspondence, slaves were instructed to obey their masters.

117

Before bidding his readers farewell, Paul exhorted them to put on the 'armour' provided by God in order that they might 'stand firm against the devices of the devil' (Ephesians 6:11). They were to put on the belt of truth, the shoes of the gospel of peace and carry the shield of faith. They were to take salvation for a helmet, and 'for sword, take that which the Spirit gives you—the words that come from God'. In this way, they would be able to stand their ground, 'to complete every task and still to stand'.

Philippians

This letter, another of the 'Captivity Letters', (Philippians 1:7), is principally concerned with personal matters. In tone it is much happier than Ephesians. It was probably dictated by Paul to Timothy and was addressed to the Christian community at Philippi and its leaders, for whom Paul shows great concern and evidently knew. He had probably stayed at Philippi for a short while on his second missionary journey (Acts 16:12), and passed through on his third missionary journey. The church there had grown strong. It appears that members of the church at Philippi had sent Epaphroditus with a contribution for Paul's upkeep while he was in prison (Philippians 2:25). Epaphroditus had stayed on to work with Paul and then become ill. Paul thanked the church at Philippi for supporting him in his missionary work, especially while he was in prison.

Paul referred to his coming trial and said that, even though he was in prison, he was happy about his situation. His imprisonment had not prevented him from preaching the gospel and this was all-important to him. He looked forward to meeting them again—if that was to be—but he was prepared to die. He **warned his readers against disunity** (Philippians 1:27—28), and, in this context, he mentioned Euodia and Syntyche (Philippians 4:2,3), two women who were evidently responsible for causing discord. Members of the church at Philippi were to set an example to others in their behaviour, shining like bright lights in the darkness of the world around. He also **warned them against Judaizers** (Philippians 3:2), who exaggerated the importance of Jewish legalism and circumcision, and **libertines** (Philippians 3:18—19), who were purely sensual people and were enemies of the Cross. In the face of such a situation they were to be steadfast in the faith.

The Pastoral Letters: 1 and 2 Timothy, Titus

These three letters contain indications of a more developed church than that suggested in the Pauline correspondence just described. For this reason, and because the words and ideas used are different, it has been suggested that the letters are the work of one of Paul's fellow-workers who may have used extracts from Paul's letters. These letters, addressed to Timothy and Titus, contain advice about the work and duties of a Christian pastor.

1 Timothy

This letter includes a warning about false teachers, two of whom are mentioned in particular. These are Hymenaeus and Alexander, who, it is said, did not understand the subject they claimed to teach. Salvation, said the author, could be gained through Christ alone. There follows what amounts to a catalogue of instructions for the pastor to relay to his congregation. Prayers were to be offered for all men, and particularly for those in authority (1 Timothy 2:1–8). Women were to show piety, to dress modestly and to be silent at worship. Their work lay in the home (1 Timothy 2:9–15). A bishop was to have one wife and to be blameless and sober (1 Timothy 3:1–7). Deacons were to be of a high standard, serious and sincere (1 Timothy 3:8–13). The church, as the pillar of Christian truth, was to be managed correctly and those charged with preaching and with the spiritual welfare of its members were to be paid. Heretical teachers whose chief interest was to make money were to be condemned.

2 Timothy

In this letter, Timothy is encouraged in his faith and is charged to pass on this faith to trusted men who, in turn, will be able to teach others. Again there is a warning about heretical teachers. In this case, they were Hymenaeus and Philetus, who were claiming that the resurrection had already taken place. Timothy was to continue to preach the Gospel and to undertake his duties to the full. The letter ends with what may be a Pauline passage, indicating that Paul was facing death.

Titus

This letter is similar to 1 Timothy and was probably intended for a number of churches. Titus was told that false teachings, especially those of Jewish origin, were to be refuted. Advice is given about Christian behaviour and teaching. Christians are to live sober and upright lives (Titus 2:11–15). The letter concerns also the appointment of presbyter-bishops whose duty was to prevent false teachings.

Chapter 7
The Bible and Current Issues

This chapter will look at a number of current problems and situations and then see what guidance the Bible has to offer people in dealing with them. For many of these situations Christians would say that the New Testament, in particular, still has relevance for them as it deals with personal relationships and these have not changed over the centuries. They would also say that the Bible can be a source of inspiration in the call for Christian action in the world today.

Personal and family issues

It is clear from a study of the Old Testament that family life was tremendously important to the people of Israel and has indeed continued to be of great importance to Judaism today. We find that, in the time of Abraham, it was from the family that the tribe and then, eventually, the nation evolved. Great emphasis was placed on the unity of the family and the respect that it should be shown. Note what the book of Exodus says about one's attitude towards parents: 'Whoever strikes his father or mother shall be put to death . . . Whoever reviles his father or mother shall be put to death ' (Exodus 21:15,17). The father ruled the household and his permission had to be sought on major issues.

As far as relationships with the opposite sex are concerned, we do not find much material in the Old Testament. We do know, however, that every endeavour was made in Old Testament times to ensure that people married within the faith and often they were condemned by the prophets for seeking wives from other countries where a different religion was practised. Abraham, for example, sent one of his stewards to Haran in the north to find a wife for his son Isaac from among his own people. When he found Rebekah she readily agreed to return with the steward to become Isaac's wife, as we saw in Chapter 1. No doubt the account as it stands is in a much simplified form but the point remains that both Isaac and Rebekah were accustomed to a situation in which marriages like this were arranged.

121

In Old Testament times, there was no question of a boyfriend/girlfriend relationship as we see today. It was very much a family affair to find a suitable partner for one's son or daughter and all those concerned respected this situation. Furthermore, there was no question of extra-marital relationships being permitted. The whole of creation and hence the family unit was divinely ordained. Adulterous behaviour such as that practised by King David with Bathsheba (2 Samuel 11:1–12:14), was condemned outright by the prophet Nathan. Divorce, too, was discouraged. The separation of the marriage partners was to part what God had expressly united: marriage was for life.

The word 'love' as used in the New Testament has several interpretations, depending on whether it is applied to people in general or to members of the opposite sex. Emphasis is placed on the need for sincerity in one's feelings. It may be claimed that love, considered in its more general sense, is really the basis of all personal relationships. Religion itself could be described as a form of love–love for God–and many have looked upon worship as love expressing itself. Love is seen as something that can achieve everything since 'there is no limit to its faith, its hope and its endurance' (I Corinthians 13:7).

We do not find specific instructions in the New Testament on the subject of personal sexual relationships, much less about the situations that beset couples today, such as birth control and abortion. This should not surprise us because the New Testament was never intended to serve as a manual for one's personal conduct, or as a guide to ethics. We do, however, find general advice about what is expected of Christians in their everyday lives. It should be borne in mind that many of the comments made about personal matters (e.g. in the letters of Paul) were written in answer to specific problems. For example, Paul had to deal with definite instances of immorality on the part of the Christian community at Corinth, and these he condemned outright. He pointed out to the church there that there should be no question of Christians committing incest (1 Corinthians 5:1–5). The person who had committed such an act was to be excluded from the church.

122

Marriage

An examination of the New Testament may suggest that it contains a contradiction concerning the importance of marriage. According to the teaching of Jesus, marriage was ordained by God at creation and was therefore to be respected. It was intended to be a happy state for the mutual enjoyment of both partners and for the purpose of continuing God's creation, as recorded in the first book of the Old Testament (Genesis 1:26–31). When Paul told his readers that it would be preferable if they did not marry, he did so in expectation of the early return of Jesus who would inaugurate the end of the age. The apparent contradiction between the teaching of Jesus and that of Paul is thus due to the difference in circumstances. Later writings of the apostle, prepared in the light of the realization that Jesus' return would not be imminent, delineate clearly the approach to be adopted by the Christian partners in marriage. They were charged to love and respect one another, becoming one flesh (Ephesians 5:31). Paul presents his readers with his version of the perfect husband/wife relationship where the husband's duty is to love his wife, and hers is to obey him. Today many people prefer to think of marriage as a partnership of equals where decisions are made jointly.

In the New Testament, sexual relationships are envisaged only within the context of marriage, where there is a firm commitment from both partners. Sex is never to be an end in itself, nor the exploitation of one partner by the other. It is to be the expression of a loving stable relationship. Extra-marital affairs are strongly condemned in the New Testament. Matthew goes further than this for he says that: 'If a man looks on a woman with a lustful eye, he has already committed adultery with her in his heart' (Matthew 5:28). Association with prostitutes is equally condemned by Paul who said that in forming a relationship with a prostitute one would be joining one's body to hers. Paul's readers were reminded that really their bodies belonged to Christ: 'Do you not know that your body is a shrine of the indwelling Holy Spirit, and the Spirit is God's gift to you?' (1 Corinthians 6:19). This should, he suggested, guide people in all their relationships, a point which is as valid today as in Paul's time.

The institution of marriage is seen as a life-long commitment in the New Testament, a permanent union of one man and one woman. This leaves no room for the 'trial' marriages and 'trial' separations of today which were unheard of in early Jewish communities. According to the New Testament writers, divorce was not permitted by Jesus, except in the case of adultery (Matthew 5:31–32). In Mark's Gospel, (Mark 10:1–9), marriage is clearly regarded as a life-long contract. Divorce was permitted by Paul in the case of a marriage between a Christian and a non-Christian where the non-Christian wanted to end the marriage (1 Corinthians 7:15). With his mind on the end of the present age, Paul gave a ruling (which he described as 'not mine but the Lord's') forbidding divorce. In the time of Paul, there was no question of a divorce being permitted, as it is today, for the irretrievable breakdown of a marriage.

We find various statements in the New Testament regarding the duties of members of a family. These passages state that they ought to love and respect one another. Paul's letter to the Ephesians is again particularly useful in this respect:

'Children obey your parents, for it is right that you should. Honour your father and mother is the first commandment with a promise attached, in the words: that it may be well with you and that you may live long in the land. You fathers, again, must not goad your children to resentment, but give them the instruction, and the correction, which belong to a Christian upbringing.'

(Ephesians 6:1–4)

The Christian was to be guided by consideration for others.

The individual in society

Work   The book of Genesis sets out quite clearly the biblical position as far as work is concerned: 'With labour you shall win your food from it [the ground] all the days of your life' (Genesis 3:17). When we look at the New Testament we find that the idea of work receives thorough approval. Jesus himself was a carpenter (Mark 6:3), and often referred to work in his parables. He described, for example, the story of the labourers in the vineyard (Matthew 20:1–16). The parable of the talents (Matthew

124

25:14–29), commands people to make the best possible use of their abilities and resources. Honesty and hard work are especially commended. Paul was a tent-maker and it seems that he always worked to support himself while on his missionary journeys. He gives himself as an example of someone who earns his living rather than being a burden on anyone (2 Thessalonians 3:7–12).

Laziness is condemned in the New Testament, especially by Paul (2 Thessalonians 3:10), as it was in the book of Proverbs (Proverbs 6:6–8, and 24:30–34). People were urged to earn their own living and work with a good will (Colossians 3:23). Work is seen by Paul as a vocation–something which provides a sense of purpose and a feeling of dignity. By working, one is making a contribution to the needs of society (1 Corinthians 12:4–11). Christians are encouraged to carry out their work willingly, cheerfully and with the right motives. They should work–as they do everything else–to please God, and not merely to earn money or satisfy their employer. Employer and employee are given guidance by Paul in their respective roles (Ephesians 6:5–9). It could be said that what Paul has to say on these matters would need to be reinterpreted today in the light of changed circumstances, but the spirit of the judgments that he made must still apply.

Use of money   The Old Testament contains many references to the use of money and emphasizes that everything, including wealth, belongs to God. Deuteronomy 8:17–18 reminds people that the strength to work and to become prosperous comes from God and should not be taken for granted. It should be borne in mind that wealth does not last forever (Proverbs 27:24) and that 'wisdom is more profitable than silver, and the gain she brings is better than gold' (Proverbs 3:13–14).

Jesus' words about those who amassed wealth can be found in Luke 12:13–34. Men and women are stewards of what God has provided for them and so money must not be misused. Yet Jesus was aware of the value of money, as can be seen from the story of the woman who looked so diligently for a lost coin (Luke 15:8–9). What Jesus wanted to emphasize was that, as shown in the Old Testament, everything, including wealth, comes from God, and that he should be thanked for it. Jesus was primarily concerned with people's attitude towards money. It should not become their God (Matthew 6:24).

Later in the New Testament we find that the author of 1 Timothy considered the love of money as the 'the root of all evil things' (1 Timothy 6:10), and leaders of the church were warned against its misuse (1 Timothy 3:3). The words of James (James 5:1–6), are devastating for those who gloat over their wealth, especially when they have not properly paid those in their employ:

> Next a word to you who have great possessions. Weep and wail over the miserable fate descending on you. Your riches have rotted; your fine clothes are moth-eaten; your silver and gold have rusted away, and their very rust will be evidence against you and consume your flesh like fire. You have piled up wealth in an age that is near its close. The wages you never paid to the men who mowed your fields are loud against you, and the outcry of the reapers has reached the ears of the Lord of Hosts. You have lived on earth in wanton luxury, fattening yourselves like cattle – and the day for slaughter has come. You have condemned the innocent and murdered him; he offers no resistance.

In contrast to this selfish use of money we find the Christian concept of sharing and giving of one's property and riches (Acts 2:44–45). This practice was adopted in the knowledge that one's true riches were to be found in heaven (1 Timothy 6:17–19).

Leisure Various passages in the Old Testament suggest that leisure time has been appointed for men and women by God. A specific day – the sabbath – was to be set aside each week as a time of complete rest, for even God himself had created the universe in six days and had rested from his labours on the seventh day (Exodus 20:8–11). Indeed, the Hebrew word 'sabbath' means 'rest'. The idea is pursued in such texts as Ecclesiastes 2:18–26, which refers to the rest after labour. The same book explains how there is a time for everything, a time set aside, ' . . . a time to seek and a time to lose; a time to keep and a time to throw away; a time to tear and a time to mend; a time for silence and a time for speech'.

Since the sabbath is ordained by God as a rest day, it is also a holy day, a sacred day on which no work is permitted. Any kind of trading and the handling of certain objects is strictly prohibited. Orthodox Jews differ, however, in their interpretation of the Jewish rules relating to the sabbath from Reform Jews who are much more likely to permit a liberal approach to what one may do on the sabbath. Despite this legal approach, Jews as a whole look to the sabbath as a day of rejoicing, of religious worship and instruction. It should be a day of refreshment to which all Jews look forward: The prophet Isaiah explains the Jewish view of the sabbath:

> If you cease to tread the sabbath underfoot, and keep my holy day from your own affairs, if you call the sabbath a day of joy and the Lord's holy day a day to be honoured, if you honour it by not plying your trade, not seeking your own interest or attending to your own affairs, then you shall find your joy in the Lord, and I will set you riding on the heights of the earth, and your father Jacob's patrimony shall be yours to enjoy; the Lord himself has spoken it.
>
> (Isaiah 58:13–14)

The New Testament has a particularly positive approach to leisure. The sabbath is regarded as a time for rest but it is also a time to attend the synagogue – as Jesus did regularly – and to think about how one might care for others. Leisure time in general is seen as an opportunity to make people whole, in body as well as in mind.

Alcohol   Wine drinking is accepted and favoured in the Old Testament, particularly as good fresh water was probably scarce (Psalms 104:15; Proverbs 9:2). The book of Ecclesiastes (Ecclesiastes 10:19), is particularly interesting on this point: 'The table has its pleasures, and wine makes a cheerful life.' The drinking of wine formed a part of Jewish worship (Numbers 15:8–10), and was used by Jews in the celebration of their festivals. The writers of the Old Testament were aware of the danger of drunkenness, however, as Hosea 4:12 and especially Isaiah 5:11 ably demonstrate. We also read of a group of people called the Nazarites who undertook a vow never to drink alcohol (Numbers 6:1–5).

127

In the New Testament we see that Jesus favoured the use of wine, as is shown by the account in John's Gospel of the wedding feast at Cana (John 2:1–11). It should also be noted how wine was an integral part of the Last Supper when Jesus took a cup of wine and blessed it and made it the symbol of his blood which was to be shed for the forgiveness of sins (Matthew 26:26–29). In the Gospels we also find a warning against drunkenness (Luke 21:34) and Paul warned his readers about the dangers of over-indulgence (1 Corinthians 11:21). The writer of 1 Timothy 5:23 is quite specific about the benefits of drinking wine: 'Stop drinking nothing but water; take a little wine for your digestion, for your frequent ailments.'

Drugs   We find no specific teaching in the New Testament about the taking of drugs. The sophisticated drugs that are supplied today were unknown to medical science in New Testament times, and there are no very clear records about the availability of drugs on the 'open market' in the time of Jesus. We are told that Jesus refused drugged wine when he was being taken to the place of crucifixion (Matthew 27:34). Paul's words to the Christians of the church of Corinth are helpful to bear in mind as they can be applied to the use of drugs or alcohol: 'Do you not know that your body is a shrine of the indwelling Holy Spirit, and the Spirit is God's gift to you?' People should not misuse their bodies or do anything that would destroy them personally or ruin their lives.

Problems of society: discrimination of class, colour and religion

What has Christianity to say about racial or any other kind of prejudice or discrimination, and what should be the Christian response to intolerance and prejudice? We could begin with the book of Genesis (Genesis 1:26), where it is said that man is made in the likeness of God, with the clear inference that all men are born equal. It was later that the Jews became concerned about the preservation of their faith and so took special measures to protect their racial and religious distinctiveness.

Nehemiah and Ezra were deeply concerned to preserve the purity of the Jewish people as a race and, as we have seen, strongly discouraged inter-marriage with people from other countries and religions. Ezra even made Jews divorce their foreign wives and husbands (Ezra 10:1–3). Quite different is the book of Ruth, which has become famous for its account of a mixed marriage between a Moabite called Ruth to Boaz an Israelite (Ruth 4:9–17). We are told that King David descended from this mixed marriage and, in due course, Jesus Christ himself descended from him. It is thus a story of some significance.

In the New Testament we find that Jesus had no time for racial discrimination or indeed discrimination of any kind. This is shown by the story of the call of Levi, the tax collector, and the fact that Jesus ate with 'tax-gatherers and sinners' (Luke 5:27–32). He showed his love for people of all nations and we find one example of this in the story of the Good Samaritan (Luke 10:30–37) which was particularly dramatic because Samaritans were disliked and despised by the Jews. On one occasion, Jesus asked a Samaritan woman if she would give him some water and then stopped to talk to her by the well. Then again, the only one of the ten lepers (Luke 17:11–19), who returned to Jesus and thanked God for healing him was a Samaritan.

The apostle Paul sought at all times to further the idea of one united community of Christian believers, as we saw in the study of the Pauline correspondence. All are sons of God (Galatians 3:20–28). There are plenty of examples in the Acts of the Apostles of how Jesus' missionaries freely spoke to and converted people of other races and thus, by implication, considered them equal in God's and man's eyes. Consider the following: Philip and the Ethiopian, a black man, (Acts 8:26–40) and Peter and the conversion of Cornelius (Acts 10:24–28). Then, in the letter to Philemon, Paul encourages Philemon to forgive Onesimus, his runaway slave, and to treat him as an equal. There is thus no doubt about Paul's view on this point: 'There is no such thing as Jew and Greek, slave and freeman, male and female; for you are all one person in Christ Jesus' (Galatians 3:28). This would seem to provide the Christian response to the situation that prevails today in some countries which practise apartheid (separation of the races). It should also provide some form of guidance to people's attitude towards immigrants.

The New Testament encourages in all cases a spirit of tolerance and understanding towards other people. It carries the inference that no discrimination should be made between people of different races, of different religions, or between men and women in general. Similarly, it implies that there should be a spirit of understanding towards people of whatever social standing. All are equal in God's sight and hence should be considered equal in all circumstances.

Law and order

The Old Testament provides us with a wealth of material regarding the manner in which the people of Israel were to conduct their lives. In this respect it must be understood that, for the Israelites, the secular and religious aspects of life were inextricably united. Indeed, for the Israelites, all aspects of life had a religious connotation in so far as everything belonged to God and he was the creator of all things. Apart from the Ten Commandments we can find innumerable laws and regulations that were built up around the religion. The first five books of the Old Testament are, in fact, called the Torah, or Law, and many of these laws can be found in Exodus, Leviticus and the book of Deuteronomy. It was hoped that no Israelite would be in doubt as to what course of action to adopt in any circumstance, so extensive was the coverage of the laws. Together with the guidelines laid down by the rabbis, these laws have been a constant help to followers of the religion down the years.

The New Testament generally assumes that one should respect the State and pay one's dues. Jesus was firm in his own commitment to leading the life of a good citizen: 'Pay Caesar what is due to Caesar' (Matthew 22:21). There was no conflict in Jesus' mind between loyalty to the state and loyalty to God, because he added ' . . . and pay God what is due to God'.

Jesus would have been familiar with the laws laid down by Moses and with the elaborations of these laws set out in the book of Deuteronomy. But he was not just concerned with the observance of laws, whether they were laws of the State or laws relating to the Jewish religion. He was above all concerned with reforming people's way of life, as the account of the woman caught in adultery indicates (John 8:3–11). He would have been more concerned with prison reform today than the retributive element of punishment. While upholding the firm framework of the law, he would have expected mercy and understanding to be shown where appropriate.

Paul was particularly proud to be a citizen of the Roman Empire and demonstrated on several occasions how valuable this was (Acts 16:37; 22:25; 25:11). He told the Christians at Rome to submit to the authorities (Romans 13:1–7), and explained why they should do so: 'There is no authority but by act of God, and the existing authorities are instituted by him.' Because this was the case, they should have no fear of the authorities.

Wealth and world poverty

There are many national and international organizations at work today whose aim it is to ensure that poor people and poor countries of the world are provided with the basic essentials to reach a satisfactory standard of living. The Salvation Army, Christian Aid, Oxfam, and the Save the Children Fund, are examples of such organizations. Some have a Christian foundation, but all are motivated by a social concern for others.

The New Testament points out that there is nothing new in poverty: the poor are always with us (Mark 14:7). Matthew 25:31–46 emphasizes one's duty to help the poor, but the New Testament takes us a stage further than this by indicating how, at the time when the Acts of the Apostles was written, many Christians were sharing their belongings (Acts 4:32). A later New Testament writing, the letter of James, points out that faith which does not lead to action is 'a lifeless thing' (James 2:17). This passage and other passages like it in the New Testament have prompted many Christians and many missionary movements to provide food and medical provisions besides spreading news of the Christian faith. Their aim has always been to help people in poorer countries to obtain a fairer share of the world's resources.

This can only take place if Christians throughout the world

131

appreciate fully the tragic circumstances in which the world's poor live. Christian agencies are therefore striving to make people in the West as aware as possible of the needs of others. Missionaries, priests and ministers find that they are having to present a new image to society as a whole. They find that they need to be public relations men and women, earnestly endeavouring to help the public appreciate how the poor live. They find that they have to be vigorous and enthusiastic when they put into action the words of Jesus regarding the Son of Man:

> For when I was hungry, you gave me food; when thirsty, you gave me drink; when I was a stranger you took me into your home, when naked you clothed me; when I was ill you came to my help, when in prison you visited me. Then the righteous will reply, 'Lord when was it that we saw you hungry and fed you, or thirsty and gave you drink, a stranger and took you home, or naked and clothed you?'. . . Anything you did for one of my brothers here, however humble, you did for me.
>
> (Matthew 25:35–40)

Evil and suffering

The idea that evil and suffering are related in some way, often directly, can be found throughout the Old Testament. Genesis chapters 3, 4 and 6–8, are concerned with man's acts of disobedience against God and the sufferings that this caused for man. According to the book of Exodus, the plagues were inflicted by God on the Egyptians because of their refusal to allow the Hebrews to leave Egypt (Exodus 7–12), and in the book of Judges (Judges 2), we read of the afflictions of the people of Israel when they worshipped other gods. The book of Job, on the other hand, is directly concerned with the sufferings of a man who fervently protested his innocence and asked God to vindicate him. Isaiah marks a turning point in Jewish thought with accounts of the sufferings of the Servant of God who suffered on behalf of others, so that in this case there was no question of suffering being punishment (Isaiah 52:13–53:12). Similarly, in the New Testament we read of the sufferings of Christ on the Cross undertaken willingly and totally for others. More recently, Maksymilian Kolbe, a Roman Catholic priest, gave his life while in a German concentration camp so that another man might live.

The idea of the Christian bearing his own cross has been a very popular concept in Christian thought. Christians can have faith that God uses evil and suffering to good effect by enabling them to achieve good out of them. Their view of suffering is thus very different from that found in the Old Testament. Instead of regarding suffering as an obstacle to faith, Christians believe that faith in Jesus Christ will eventually overcome evil. For example, Christians believe that their faith in God will support them in the face of death, so that they will regard this prospect calmly, rather than with fear.

War and peace

'In days to come', says the book of Micah in the Old Testament, 'the mountain of the Lord's house shall be set over all other mountains, lifted high above the hills.' At this time 'nation shall not lift sword against nation nor ever again be trained for war . . . ' (Micah 4:1,3). Many wars have been waged since the writing of this book, however, and many lives have been lost as a result. Today the outlook is overshadowed by the threat of nuclear destruction.

Matthew 5:38–48 has often been taken to suggest that Christians should adopt a pacifist stance in the face of attack and war. Yet Christians have often found themselves asking whether freedom and the defence of principles are more important than peace. The Christian religion has been responsible for many 'just' wars such as the Crusades. Today, as much as at any time in the past, Christians find themselves with a problem: should they follow the teaching of Jesus as it is given in Matthew's Gospel, or resort to force to protect their ideals?

Part Two
World Religions in Practice Today

Chapter 8
Judaism

Jewish writings

The Jewish scriptures are written in Hebrew and consist of twenty-four books which can be divided into three sections:

1. **The Law Books (the Torah)**   This section consists of: Genesis, Exodus, Leviticus, Numbers and Deuteronomy. They are often referred to as the books of Moses, though it is generally assumed that they were written by scribes long after the death of Moses. This is the most important section.

2. **The Prophets**   These eight books are divided into two sections: the **Former Prophets** (Joshua, Judges, Samuel and Kings) and the **Latter Prophets** (Isaiah, Jeremiah, Ezekiel and the twelve minor prophets Hosea, Joel, Amos, Obadiah, Jonah, Micah, Nahum, Habakkuk, Zephaniah, Haggai, Zechariah and Malachi). The twelve minor prophets count as one book.

3. **The Writings** consist of eleven books: Psalms, Proverbs, Job, The Song of Solomon, Ruth, Lamentations, Ecclesiastes, Esther, Ezra-Nehemiah, Chronicles and Daniel.

In addition to these books, there is a collection of writings which is not included in the Jewish scriptures and this is called the **Apocrypha**.

Jews believe that Moses was given two Torahs–the 'Written Torah' described above and the 'Oral Torah', handed down from generation to generation. This consisted of extremely detailed rules and regulations relating to every aspect of Jewish life, and was eventually written down to ensure that it would be accurately preserved. It is known as the **Mishnah**. The Mishnah was the subject of much study and discussion by the rabbis, and the teachings which resulted, called the **Gemara**, were added to the Mishnah and the complete work was called the **Talmud**.

Jewish beliefs and teachings

Jewish beliefs are best considered by studying the Ten Commandments as set out in Exodus 20:1–17 and Deuteronomy

5:6–21, and by examining the Thirteen Principles of the Jewish scholar, Moses Maimonides, who lived 800 years ago.

The Thirteen Principles of Maimonides
1. God exists.
2. There is only one God.
3. He has no body and so is not limited like men.
4. He is eternal.
5. Jews should pray only to him.
6. The teachings of the prophets are true.
7. Moses was the greatest of the prophets.
8. The teachings of Moses were revealed to him by God.
9. The Law is God's final word.
10. God knows everything.
11. God rewards the good and punishes the evil.
12. The messiah is expected.
13. The dead will be resurrected.

Initiation ceremonies: circumcision and bar mitzvah

It is customary for all Jewish boys to be **circumcised** on the eighth day after birth. This means that the foreskin of the penis is cut away. It is a small operation, usually performed by a trained person, and carried out in accordance with Genesis 17:10–12.

When a Jewish boy reaches the age of thirteen, he is declared to be an adult as far as the Jewish religion is concerned. He is **bar (son of) mitzvah (the commandment)**, and is eligible to read from the scroll in the synagogue on the sabbath nearest to his thirteenth birthday. On this day he may put on his **tefillin** for the first time. This is a small black box with a long strap containing passages from the Law of Moses. It is worn on the left arm facing the heart. Another tefillin is worn on the forehead. These are worn to remind Jews of the Law, which must always be in their hearts and in their minds (Deuteronomy 6:4–9). He will also wear his **tallith**, or prayer shawl, and his skull cap, or **yarmulka**.

Jewish worship

The Jewish home is a focal point for prayer and the celebration of the sabbath. There are three fixed periods of prayer at home or in the synagogue–morning, afternoon and evening–corresponding with the hours of sacrifice in the Temple. Even before he enters the home a Jew is reminded of the presence of God by the **mezuzah**, a small box usually positioned in an elevated position on the right hand side of the doorpost. The word 'mezuzah' in fact means 'doorpost'. Like the tefillin, it contains passages from the Old Testament.'

The **sabbath**, or Jewish day of rest, is celebrated in the home with the whole family present. The sabbath begins on Friday evening at sunset and extends to sunset on Saturday. During this period, Jews must do no work but devote the time to prayer, study and rest (Exodus 20:8–11):

> Remember to keep the sabbath day holy. You have six days to labour and do all your work. But the seventh day is a sabbath of the Lord your God; that day you shall not do any work, you, your son or your daughter, your slave or your slave girl, your cattle or the alien within your gates; for in six days the Lord made heaven and earth, the sea, and all that is in them, and on the seventh day he rested. Therefore the Lord blessed the sabbath and declared it holy.
>
> (Exodus 20:8–11)

Orthodox Jewish fathers and their sons go to the synagogue on the evening of the sabbath while the wife lights the candles to begin the sabbath celebrations in the home. The sabbath is intended to be an opportunity to relax and sing songs together, remembering that it is the Lord's day, a holy day. One of the most cherished blessings is recited by the father on this day to his children: 'The Lord bless thee and keep thee; the Lord make his face shine upon thee, and give thee peace.'

When at least ten Jewish men are present, a service may be held at a synagogue, or house of assembly. The synagogue may also be used as a meeting-place and a school for the teaching of Hebrew. Except in Reform synagogues, women do not generally take an active part in synagogue worship.

Those attending a service sit in pews facing the **Ark**, which is a cupboard on the wall nearest Jerusalem, and which contains one or more copies of the Pentateuch written in Hebrew. Above it is usually positioned a plaque on which the Ten Comnmandments are written. There may also be a lamp above the Ark. This is always lit, as in the days of the Temple at Jerusalem. Nearby is a seven-branched candlestick, called a **menorah**. In the centre of the synagogue is the **bimah**, a raised reading desk, where the president of the assembly conducts the service. In orthodox synagogues, men and women are seated separately.

Wearing their skull caps and prayer shawls, male members of the congregation sing psalms from the Hebrew Prayer Book. This is followed by the **Shema**, quoted in Chapter One, and which is also in the tefillin and mezuzah. This is recited daily by all Jews. They then stand for the **Amidah** prayer, which consists of eighteen blessings. The Ark is then solemnly opened and one of the scrolls of the Law is removed and carried round the synagogue. There is a reading from it in the original Hebrew, and then the scroll is carried round the synagogue once more; those present may touch it with the fringes of their talliths: they then kiss the fringe. Passages from the Prophets which have some link with the reading from the Law are then read, and a sermon is preached by the rabbi.

Fasts and festivals

The Jewish year starts with **Rosh Hashanah**, in September or October. This is a day of penitence when it is emphasized that the whole world stands under the judgment of God. Jews are called on to express sorrow for all they have done wrong during the past year. They gather in the synagogue, and the morning service is introduced by the blowing of a ram's horn, the **shofar**. This has rich associations, and is a reminder, among other things, of Abraham's sacrifice of the ram instead of his son, Isaac, and of the Covenant given on Mount Sinai. Special blessings are read.

Rosh Hashanah is the first of ten days of repentance which lead up to the fast of **Yom Kippur**, otherwise known as the **Day of Atonement**. This is a day of penitence and abstinence for all adult Jews. It is the holiest day of the Jewish year when five services are held in the synagogue. The constant theme of Yom Kippur is the duty to return to God in confession, repentance and desire to amend. The afternoon service is inspired by the book of Jonah, where God withholds punishment from the people of Nineveh because of their repentance. It is emphasized that atonement is available for everyone. The Day of Atonement ends at sunset with a service recalling the closing of the Temple gates. At the end, the congregation repeats seven times 'The Lord, he is God'–the words with which the people of Israel acclaimed the triumph of the prophet Elijah over the prophets of Baal on Mount Carmel. One long blast of the Shofar in front of the Ark marks the end of the day.

Five days later comes **Succoth**, or the **Feast of Tabernacles**, or **Booths**, which is one of the Pilgrim Festivals (Leviticus 23:39–43). This festival reminds Jews of the time their ancestors lived in tents in the wilderness. Many Jewish families make tents open to the sky in their gardens, where they eat their meals during the festival.

Chanucah (or **Hannukah**), means 'consecration', and is also called the **Festival of Light**. It is an eight-day festival and reminds Jews of the occasion when Judas Maccabeus 'cleansed' the Temple which the king Antiochus Epiphanes had desecrated in 165 BC. For some time before this, Jews had been forbidden to practise their religion. When Judas entered the Temple, he found oil for the sanctuary lamp sufficient to last for one day only but, miraculously, it lasted eight days. For this reason a special eight-branched candlestick is used in Jewish homes at this time of year and a candle is lit on each of the eight nights of the festival.

At the time of **Purim** (also called the **Feast of Lots**) in February/March, Jews celebrate the occasion when Esther, the Jewish wife of Xerxes, King of Persia, prevented Haman, one of the emperor's ministers, from putting the Jews to death in Persia. Haman had decided by lots on which day the Jews would be put to death but in the end it was Haman who met his death.

Pesach, or **Passover**, another of the Pilgrim festivals, is the main Jewish festival and lasts eight days during March or April. At this time Jews remember the occasion of the Exodus when the Hebrews in Egypt marked their door-posts with the blood of a lamb so that the angel of death would pass over them (Exodus

139

12:27). They also remember the last meal they had before they escaped from Egypt when they ate unleavened bread because they had no time for the yeast to rise. For this reason no leavened bread is allowed in a Jewish house at Passover time.

Jews celebrate the occasion with a special meal in the home which consists of:
- a roast sheep bone, which represents the Passover lamb;
- a roasted egg, to represent the hope of a new life (neither the bone nor the egg is eaten);
- nuts and raisins to represent the mortar which the Hebrew slaves used when building with bricks;
- bitter herbs to represent the misery of slavery;
- green vegetables to represent the goodness of God in providing them with food;
- salt water which represents the tears that their ancestors shed while they were slaves;
- unleavened bread to remind them of the haste with which their ancestors left Egypt.

Three pieces of unleavened bread lie in front of the head of the house, representing the priests, the Levites and people of Israel. The middle one is broken and part is eaten at the end of the meal. The head of the house says 'This is the bread of affliction that our fathers ate in the land of Egypt. Let all who are hungry come and eat. Let all who are in want come and celebrate the Passover with us.' At this point, the youngest child present asks 'Why is this night different from all other nights?' in response to which the story of the Israelites' captivity in Egypt and their deliverance by God is dramatically told.

Jews drink four glasses of wine during the meal to remind them of the four promises made by God to redeem Israel (Exodus 6:6–7). They place one cup of wine on the table for the prophet Elijah. The service ends with the psalms of Hallel (praise), Psalms 113–118, and the final cup of wine and a blessing.

Shavuot, or the **Feast of Weeks**, which is also called **Pentecost**, is the third Pilgrim festival, and takes place seven weeks after the festival of Passover. On this occasion Jews celebrate the giving of the Law to Moses on Mount Sinai. At this time the synagogue may be decorated with flowers and fruit.

Special food customs

There are many special food customs relating to food and how it is prepared. Meat and dairy food must be kept separate in the preparation stages and the utensils in which they are cooked must be washed up separately. The blood of any animal must be drained away before it is eaten, according to an Old Testament regulation (Leviticus 17:12). Jews may eat only animals that have cloven hoofs and chew the cud. Pork, for instance, is forbidden, and so are birds of prey and fish without fins and scales. The animal to be eaten must be killed by a Jewish butcher to render it **'kosher'** (proper) food.

Chapter 9
Christianity

Christian Scriptures

The Christian Bible consists of the **Old Testament**, which, as we have seen, was written in Hebrew and forms the basis of the Jewish faith, and the **New Testament**, which consists of twenty-seven books written in Greek by early followers of the Christian faith. In the Christian version of the Old Testament there are thirty-nine books, as 1 and 2 Samuel, 1 and 2 Kings, 1 and 2 Chronicles, Ezra and Nehemiah, and each of the minor prophets are counted separately.

The New Testament consists of:
– the four Gospels (Matthew, Mark, Luke, and John);
– The Acts of the Apostles;
– the Letters (Romans, 1 and 2 Corinthians, Galatians, Ephesians, Philippians, Colossians, 1 and 2 Thessalonians, 1 and 2 Timothy, Titus, Philemon, Hebrews, James, 1 and 2 Peter, 1, 2, and 3 John, and Jude);
– The Revelation of John.

The church fairly quickly agreed that most of these books were **canonical** (authoritative) and composed a standard 'list' or 'canon'. It was the fourth century, however, before the full collection was agreed. Even in the second century AD, these books were being translated from Greek into other languages, and in the course of the centuries, the New Testament has been made available in over a thousand languages. Familiar English versions, that is translations, are the so-called Authorized Version of 1611, the Revised Standard Version of 1946, and the New English Version which appeared in 1961.

Christian beliefs and teachings

There are many denominations within Christianity and it is not easy to formulate or categorize beliefs and teachings in any detailed form that would apply to all of them. It is possible, however, to set out certain fundamental beliefs. Christians accept that Jesus is the Son of God, that he is one with God the Father who created all things, and that he rose from the dead. They believe that Jesus was the Christ, the 'Anointed One', the messiah promised by God to bring about the Kingdom of Heaven on earth. They believe that, by dying on the Cross, he took upon himself the sins of the world, so that those who believed in him would not suffer eternal separation from God but would have everlasting life with him. They consider that, through the Holy Spirit, God's work continues here on earth.

Of the various Creeds (statements of belief in the Christian faith) the Apostles' Creed has become generally accepted in the West.

The Apostles' Creed
I believe in God the Father Almighty,
Maker of heaven and earth:
And in Jesus Christ his only Son our Lord,
Who was conceived by the Holy Ghost,
Born of the Virgin Mary,
Suffered under Pontius Pilate,
Was crucified, dead and buried,
He descended into hell;
The third day he rose again from the dead,
He ascended into heaven,
And sitteth on the right hand of God the Father Almighty;
From thence he shall come to judge the quick and the dead.
I believe in the Holy Ghost,
The Holy Catholic Church,
The Communion of Saints,
The Forgiveness of sins,
The Resurrection of the body,
And the Life everlasting.

Initiation ceremonies: Baptism and Confirmation

Most churches have **infant baptism** where parents and godparents make certain promises on the child's behalf and undertake to bring the child up to understand fully the teachings of the church. When a child is baptized, or, as it is said, 'christened' (usually in church at a font) water is sprinkled on his forehead and the priest makes the sign of the Cross over him. At this time the child is given his Christian name. Baptism may take place during one of the regular Sunday services or perhaps on a Sunday afternoon with just the relatives and friends present.

Some Christian groups, such as the Baptists, practise **'believers' baptism'** by full immersion, as they believe that one cannot fully commit oneself to Christ unless one is consciously believing. In this case there may be a special pool in the church, or, alternatively, baptism may take place in a stream, a river, or in the sea, as was practised in the early church. The Free Churches today have a service when instead of being baptized, a child is dedicated to Christ. The Methodist and United Reformed churches, as well as the Scottish Presbyterians, have infant baptism.

At a later stage, usually during their teens, young people may attend a **Confirmation** service at their local church. On this occasion they 'confirm' that they are prepared to follow the teachings of the church. Each candidate for confirmation is asked three questions by the bishop: 'Do you turn to Christ?' 'Are you sorry for your sins?', and 'Do you turn away from sin?' The candidate answers the bishop who places his hand on the young person's head and gives him his blessing.

Christian worship

Sunday was chosen as the Christian day of worship because it was the day on which Jesus rose from the dead. On this day, Christians meet in churches, chapels, or mission halls, to sing, pray, and worship God.

Churches are often built in the shape of a cross with the entrance at the west end. At the east end of the church is the **sanctuary** where the altar, or communion table is situated. Often a cross is placed on the altar. There may be a choir robed in cassocks and surplices seated in the part of the church in front of the sanctuary, called the **chancel**. From this point the priest (in Roman Catholic or Anglican churches) or the minister (in the Free Churches) conducts the service. The congregation, men and women, sit in the main part of the church which is called the **nave**. All Christian church services

144

are congregational in nature, that is to say, all those present take a full part in the worship.

The **Holy Communion**, or **Eucharist**, (thanksgiving), is the main service in the Anglican, Roman Catholic, and Greek and Russian Orthodox Churches. The service may also be called **Mass**, or **the Lord's Supper**, or **the Breaking of Bread**, as in some of the Free Churches. It is a service patterned upon Jesus' Last Supper with his disciples, just before he was arrested. As Jesus handed them the bread and the wine, he said (according to Mark 14:22, 24), 'Take this, this is my body,' and 'This is my blood, the blood of the covenant, shed for many.' These words are recited by the priest or minister as the members of the congregation receive a small piece of bread and sip of wine.

In addition to the Communion Service, most churches have a morning service of worship, known in the Anglican church as **Mattins**. During this service, hymns or psalms are sung, accompanied by an organ or piano or sometimes by guitars and other musical instruments. There are Old Testament and New Testament readings, often delivered from a lectern by a member of the congregation rather than the priest or minister, and prayers are said in praise of God. These may be prayers of adoration, confession, intercession or petition, demonstrating the variety of ways in which people need God. The **Creed** is recited as a statement of belief and a sermon or address is given by the priest or minister, usually based on or prefaced by a text from the Bible. This may be delivered from a pulpit. The service ends with a blessing, or benediction, given only by the priest. There is a similar service known as **Evensong** in the Church of England and Evening Worship in other denominations.

Fasts and festivals

The Church Year begins at **Advent**, four Sundays before Christmas. At this time Christians prepare for Jesus' birth celebrated on 25th December. The word 'Advent' comes from a Latin word *adventus*, which means 'coming', and so is used to refer to the coming of Christ. In the West, Advent Sunday is always the Sunday nearest to St Andrew's Day (30 November). In the past, it was a period of penitence and therefore of fasting. Today, however, Advent is no longer marked by fasting but maintains its importance as a time when Christians can ensure that they are in the right frame of mind for the coming of Jesus. At **Christmas** Christians everywhere celebrate the coming of Jesus and the message of peace and goodwill to all men. A special communion service is held in many churches, called the Midnight Mass, and on Christmas Day presents are exchanged between friends and relatives. Many churches build a small crib representing the stable in which Jesus was born, with figures of him as a baby and his parents, Mary and Joseph, and the animals looking on.

Christmas is followed by **Epiphany** on 6th January. The word 'Epiphany' comes from a Greek word meaning 'manifestation' or 'appearance'. This special occasion finds its origin in the East where it was associated with the baptism of Jesus. In the West, it became associated with the appearance of Christ to the Gentiles by means of the Magi (the Wise Men from the East who were guided to the baby Jesus). It is thus a season connected with the mission of Christianity to the whole world so that all might believe in Jesus. It signifies the taking of the light of Christmas into the world.

The period of **Lent** is introduced by **Ash Wednesday**, when palms given to members of the congregation the previous year on Palm Sunday are burnt. Lent extends over the six weeks leading up to Easter and is traditionally a period of penance and fasting. At this time, Christians remember how Jesus spent forty days in the wilderness and was tempted by the devil. **Palm Sunday** introduces Holy Week and commemorates the day Jesus entered Jerusalem and was greeted by disciples and other followers who threw down palm branches in front of him (John 12:13). For this reason, palms are distributed in church on this day. **Good Friday** commemorates the day Jesus was crucified. Many churches hold a special service which may last for as long as three hours since this was the time Jesus is said to have suffered on the Cross. Crosses may be covered in black or removed from the church.

Easter Day is a moveable feast which is traditionally based on the

146

date of the Jewish Passover and is the most important of the Christian festivals. It takes place in March or April when Christians celebrate the resurrection of Jesus from the dead. This is seen by Christians as a mighty act of God who raised Jesus up and placed him at his right hand in a position of honour (Acts 2:22–36). Christ was victorious over death and brought the opportunity of a new life to his followers. The season thus signifies the beginning of a new era, a new beginning for all believers in Christ. Christians celebrate the occasion by giving one another chocolate Easter eggs which symbolize the beginning of a new life.

Ascension Day, when Jesus ascended into heaven, falls on the Thursday following the fourth Sunday after Easter. At **Whitsuntide**, or Pentecost, seven Sundays after Easter, Christians celebrate the day the disciples received the power of the Holy Spirit. This day is usually referred to as the birthday of the Christian church. On the Sunday after Whitsunday, called **Trinity**, the church remembers the threefold nature of the Godhead, Father, Son and Holy Spirit.

Christian pilgrimages

The idea of visiting holy places as a pilgrimage is widespread within Christianity, particularly in the Anglican and Roman Catholic traditions. In 1858, Bernadette Soubirous received eighteen visions of the Virgin Mary at **Lourdes**, in France, and since then, many Roman Catholics each year have made a pilgrimage to the Grotto of Massabiele in the hope of being cured of their infirmities. Bernadette Soubirous later became a nun and was canonized in 1933. Roman Catholics also go on pilgrimages to **Fatima** in Portugal, and **Knock**, in the Republic of Ireland.

Members of the Anglican Church have a number of famous holy places in England and Scotland, such as **Glastonbury, Canterbury, Walsingham, Lindisfarne and Holy Island**. **Jerusalem**, in a sense the home of Christianity, and **Rome**, which soon became the centre of the Western Church, are regularly visited by Christian pilgrims. Christianity today is a highly organized religion, having a membership covering the whole of the Western World.

Chapter 10
Islam

Muhammad the Prophet

Muhammad was born in Mecca in AD 570, and, after the death of his parents, he was brought up by his uncle Abu Talib. When he was twenty-five he married Khadija, a rich widow, for whom he had worked as a trading agent. He soon became **dissatisfied with the life and conditions of the people around him in Mecca**. He was especially unhappy at the **polytheism** of the people who worshipped the images of the gods in the Ka'ba, a cube-shaped building, thirty feet high, thirty-five feet long and thirty feet wide, which, according to tradition, was built by Abraham and Ishmael, ancestors of the Arabs. The people of Mecca especially revered the Black Stone which lay in one corner of the Ka'ba and which may have been a meteorite that fell to earth before Muhammad's time. Muhammad was also unhappy about the many **social injustices** prevalent at the time, such as the treatment of the poor, widows and orphans, the status of women and the plight of slaves.

He began visiting a cave near Mecca so that he could meditate alone. It was here that, at the age of forty, he received a vision from the angel Gabriel who told him to recite what he said:

> In the name of God the Merciful, the Compassionate,
> Recite: In the name of thy Lord who created,
> created Man of a blood-clot.
> Recite: And thy Lord is the Most Generous,
> who taught by the Pen,
> taught Man that he knew not.

This passage now forms part of the 96th chapter, or sura, of the Qur'an. As a result of the vision, Muhammad realized that his mission was to **preach to his people and tell them to reform their religion**. Somewhat startled, Muhammad reported all that he had heard and seen to his wife, Khadija, who listened carefully to what he told her and encouraged him in his work. In AD 160, he preached to the Meccans about **Allah, the one God**, and urged them to change their ways. Perhaps not surprisingly, his message was not well received. Indeed, he was ridiculed and abused and left Mecca for

Yathrib, which was two hundred miles to the north of Mecca. This city was later called Medina, the city of the prophet, after Muhammad was made its leading citizen. The now famous departure from Mecca is called the **'hijra'**, that is 'emigration'. In AD 630, after a series of battles, Muhammad returned and took Mecca, destroying the images of the gods in the Ka'ba. He died two years later in AD 632 and was succeeded by a series of 'caliphs', or 'successors'.

Islamic writings: The Qur'an (or Koran), and the Hadith

The **Qur'an** is the holy book of Islam and consists of the words of Allah as revealed to Muhammad over a period of some twenty years. The word 'Qur'an' means 'recitation' and the revelations are believed to be the actual word of God. Muhammad had memorized all of these revelations since he could neither read nor write. His followers wrote them down on 'Scraps of parchment and leather, tablets of stone, ribs of palm branches, camels' shoulder-blades and ribs, pieces of board and on the breasts of men'. The first copy of the Qur'an, in Arabic, was not written down until after Muhammad's death. It consists of 114 suras, the longest placed first.

The book maintains **the existence of one God, Allah,** in contrast to the belief in many gods held at that time. In this book, there are rules about the Islamic faith, and especially about prayer. There are **strict guidelines about all social relationships**, such as marriage and divorce, rules about **how to conduct one's business affairs**, and warnings about **the certainty of God's judgment** on the people. On that day everyone will be called to account for his actions. Hell is depicted in dramatic terms.

Many Muslims learn the Qur'an by heart and great merit is attached to this accomplishment. The Qur'an is treasured as the word of God by all followers of the faith and when not in use it is placed on a shelf and is covered with a cloth. No other book is allowed to be placed on top of it.

The **Hadith**, or 'tradition', is a collection of **the sayings of Muhammad**. They form an elaboration of or commentary on the teachings found in the Qur'an. Unlike the Qur'an, there are many versions of the Hadith.

The Five Pillars of Islam
There are five religious duties of a Muslim which are known as the Five Pillars:
1. **Shahada** (Creed)   Every Muslim must accept and recite the statement that there is no God but Allah and that Muhammad is his prophet:
> In the name of God, the Merciful, the Compassionate,
> Say, He is God, One,
> God the Everlasting Refuge,
> who has not begotten, and has not been begotten,
> and equal to Him is not any one.
>
> (sura 92)

Muslims believe that, though God is unknowable, he is nearer to man than his own jugular vein.
2. **Salat** (prayer)   Muslims must pray five times a day: when rising, at noon, in the afternoon, at sunset, and on going to bed. They kneel on a prayer-mat, facing Mecca, and offer their prayers in Arabic. They do so in the knowledge that they are forming part of a great brotherhood of believers. In addition to these formal times for prayers, Muslims may offer supplementary prayers at any time of the day.
3. **Saum** (fasting)   All Muslims must fast from dawn to dusk of each day during the month of Ramadan. This reminds them what it is like to be poor.
4. **Zakat** (gift-offering)   All Muslims are expected to give 2½% of their income to the poor. Again, as with fasting, this is intended to remind them of the condition of the poor.
5. **Hajj** (pilgrimage)   At least once in a lifetime Muslims of all nationalities must make the pilgrimage to Mecca, after which they may place the word 'hajj' in front of their name.

Place of worship: the mosque
The word 'mosque' means 'a place of prostration'. The mosque is usually a rectangular building, not necessarily roofed, to which Muslims come to pray. It is here also that Muslim children are

150

taught the Qur'an. In Western countries, the mosque may be any building adapted for Muslim worship. In Muslim countries, one may hear the **muezzin**, the prayer caller, summoning the faithful to prayer from the balcony of the minaret, a tall tower attached to the mosque. Muslim women usually remain at home to pray, whereas Muslim men gather at the mosque on Fridays at midday. They remove their shoes at the entrance and cover their heads with a skull-cap. There are no seats in a mosque. Kneeling on their prayer mats, they face in the direction of Mecca, as indicated by a mihrab, a recess in the wall. There are no images or pictures in a mosque as Islam does not permit any pictorial representation of God.

Worship takes the form of a series of prayers. These are led by the **Imam** (prayer-leader) who may be any member of the local Muslim community. The prayer movements, or **'raka's'**, are as follows:
1. The Muslim raises his hands to each side of his face.
2. He crosses his hands in front and raises them to the side of his face again.
3. He bows and raises himself.
4. He prostrates himself on the floor twice.
5. He sits down on his heels between each of these prostrations.
6. He turns his head to the right and to the left.
These movements are accompanied by recitations from the Qur'an.

Fasts and festivals
We have already seen how important **Ramadan** is for Muslims and how they fast throughout the month. During this month, Muslims must not eat or drink anything until nightfall. They may not even smoke a cigarette. Exceptions are made for the sick and pregnant women. There is also understanding for those who are on a journey. The Qur'an provides specific guidelines on the right course of action for all believers:

> You who believe, fasting has been prescribed for you, just as it was prescribed for those before you, so that you may do your duty on days that have been fixed. Any of you who is ill or on a journey should choose a number of other days. For those who can afford it, making up for it means feeding a

poor man; if someone offers even more, it is better for him; although it is better for you to fast.

(sura 2:183–184)

It provides the Muslim with a period of discipline which he undergoes willingly.

At the end of the month of Ramadan comes the festival of **Id-al-Fitre**, also called the 'small festival'. This lasts three days and is a time for visiting friends and sending one another cards. The poor are not forgotten; it is customary to send them food.

Id-al-Adha, also called the great festival, lasts four days and begins at the end of the pilgrimage to Mecca. At this time Muslims remember how, according to their tradition, Ishmael, Abraham's son, was nearly sacrificed. For those who are taking part in the pilgrimage, the festival takes place at the village of Mina, where pilgrims make an animal sacrifice. Once again, it is an opportunity for giving to the poor.

The pilgrimage to Mecca

The pilgrimage to Mecca, as we have seen, is one of the religious duties of every Muslim. It is also something to which every Muslim eagerly looks forward. To visit the **Ka'ba** in the holy city of Islam is, for the faithful, a life's ambition.

When they arrive at the city of Mecca, all pilgrims wear a white seamless garment, called the Ihram and they walk barefoot. This is intended to demonstrate the equality of all Muslims before God. There is a special programme of events:

1. First, all pilgrims pass round the Ka'ba seven times–three times quickly and four times slowly–in an anti-clockwise direction, kissing or touching the black stone as they pass.

2. They then pass between the hills Safa and Marwa seven times, remembering Ishmael's mother, Hagar, who ran between the hills looking for water. Ishmael found a spring, which is now called Zam-Zam.

3. They proceed to mount Arafat, thirteen miles away where they offer prayers.

4. At Mina, a small village, stones are thrown at a pillar. Pilgrims remember how the devil tried to tempt Ishmael to turn against his father when he was about to sacrifice him and how he threw stones at the devil to frighten him away. A sacrifice of a sheep is made here just as Abraham offered a sheep to God instead of Ishmael.
5. On returning to Mecca, pilgrims pass round the Ka'ba again.

Chapter 11
Hinduism

The word 'Hinduism' originally referred to a region, a land around the Indus River. There was no one single person responsible for the founding of the religion, which began to develop about 1500 BC. Tradition suggests that a number of **'rishis'**, or wise men, recorded their beliefs in Sanskrit, a language which is no longer spoken but used only in Hindu worship.

Hindu writings

For many years sacred Hindu teachings were learnt and passed on orally. Some centuries later they were written down. Basically, they consist of two types of literature: **'sruti'**, or 'revealed scriptures', that is writings that were revealed to the rishis by the gods, and **'smrti'**, or 'remembered' scriptures.

The **revealed scriptures** consist of the **Vedas** and the **Upanishads**. The four books called the Vedas are hymns addressed to the gods and goddesses, the ancient nature dieties. They were composed about 1500–500 BC, and are thus the most ancient and hence the most sacred of Hindu books. The Upanishads are commentaries on the Vedas made by the wise men and were composed about 800–500 BC. Here we read that the many gods mentioned in the Vedas are really one god called **Brahman**, who is the spiritual power behind them all. It is here that we read of reincarnation and the law of **karma**, that is, the idea that good actions will bring about a good rebirth and bad actions a bad rebirth.

The **'remembered' writings** consist of the two Epics, that is the **Mahabharata** and the **Ramayana**, together with the **Laws of Manu** and the **Puranas**. The Epic **Mahabharata** is concerned with stories of the gods and ancient heroes of India and was written down between 400 BC and 300 AD. It is the world's longest poem. The Mahabharata includes the famous **Bhagavad-Gita**, that is 'The Song of the Lord', which is about Lord Krishna, an avatar (earthly form) of a god. It explains his teaching to the warrior prince

Arjuna, and shows how the way of devotion to a particular god is open to all men and women. It was included in the Mahabharata about the first century AD. The **Ramayana** is said to be written by a certain poet called Valmiki between AD 100 and 200 and tells the story of Prince Rama, an avatar of the god Vishnu: it provides us with a picture of heroic behaviour. The **Laws of Manu** are rules about many aspects of life, showing how people should lead their lives. It was written about 200 BC, by one of the rishis. The **Puranas** are collections of ancient myths and legends of the gods and goddesses, stories which have accumulated over the centuries, so that no Purana has a single author or precise date.

Beliefs and teachings

The term 'Hinduism' covers a multitude of beliefs and practices and it is impossible to do justice to them all in such a short section as this. However, it could be said that, in general, Hindus believe that there is a **Universal Spirit**, whom they call **Brahman**, who is all things and which is in all things. Brahman is the unchanging reality which is in all things yet is not subject to change. The diversity of the material world obscures this hidden reality and so the world is regarded as **maya**, less than real, an illusion. The goal is to be released from the cycle of rebirth and absorbed into Brahman. Brahman cannot be **known but can be worshipped through other gods, such as Brahma, the Creator, Vishnu, the Preserver, and Shiva, the Destroyer**. It is believed that Vishnu has appeared on earth in different forms (avatars) many times before, two of which (Krishna and Rama) were mentioned in the previous section.

Hindus today may worship hundreds of gods or none. Two most important aspects of Hinduism, however, are that one should **pursue the truth and practise harmlessness**, called **'ahimsa'**. Some Hindus seek the truth by practising meditation in the form of yoga. The practitioner attempts to seek union with the Absolute (Brahman).

A Hindu may seek to pass through the **four stages of life**, called **'ashramas'**. This means that he first becomes a **student** and learns parts of the Vedas. In the next stage he becomes a **householder** and cares for his family. In middle age he may become a **forest dweller** with his wife and lead a life of meditation. Then finally, there is a stage (reached by few Hindus) when one may become a **wanderer** and forsake all worldly ties to wander from place to place.

The idea of **reincarnation** is never far away from the Hindu mind. He will constantly be aware that his present actions will affect the nature of his next life in this world, which takes place quite automatically. This concept is known as **karma**. A person's bad deeds build up his karma so the Hindu aims to live in such a way that he has as little karma as possible so that he will earn a better rebirth even if he does not achieve **moksha** (salvation, release from the wheel of life). He feels bound to the **wheel of life (samsara)**, which signifies birth, death and rebirth. He may be reborn as another human being, or indeed, as an animal if his actions in his present life warrant such 'demotion'. He may otherwise be relegated to another caste, as there is a two-way movement in this respect. Importance is still attached today to the **caste system** despite moves to dissolve it. A Hindu may be born a **Brahmin** (a member of the priestly caste), a **Kshatriya** (a ruler warrior), or a **Vaishya** (a tradesman or craftsman). These three castes are called 'twice-born', as they are entitled to undergo the ceremony of the sacred thread. After these castes come the **Shudras** (manual workers), the lowest caste. A further group, the **untouchables**, are outcasts or 'pariahs'.

Initiation into Hinduism

There are sixteen stages in the life of a Hindu, with a ritual attached to each. Of particular importance is the ceremony that takes place when a Hindu child is born. The sacred word **'Om'** or **'Aum'** is written on its tongue with a golden pen dipped in honey. The child is named later. Every Hindu child has his first hair cut off which symbolizes the removal of bad karma (actions), from his former life.

Another stage takes place some years later when the guru, or religious teacher, places the **sacred thread of the twice-born** over the child's left shoulder and lets it hang over the right side. As indicated, this ceremony takes place only for members of the Brahmin, Kshatriya and Vaishya castes. The candidate for initiation, who may be a teenager, then becomes the guru's pupil and studies the sacred Hindu writings under him.

Hindu worship

Every Hindu home will have a puja room or a puja shelf. The word **'puja'** means worship and the special room or shelf is set aside for the images of the gods, such as Rama and Krishna. These gods are worshipped daily with offerings of food and flowers. The worshipper enters the room in the morning, having first removed his shoes. The god is wakened and dressed; later in the day it is undressed. Incense in the form of joss sticks may be used to assist meditation. Private worship like this is quite usual for the Hindu since worship is essentially an individual practice; each Hindu has to achieve **moksha** (salvation) separately, though Hindus do meet collectively for worship in the most colourfully decorated temples called **mandirs**.

There is no set day for worship in Hinduism, though it is usual for Hindus to meet in the local mandir on a Sunday. They remove their shoes on entering the puja room. They present an offering to the gods, who are cared for by the temple priests, and then sit down on the floor as there are no seats in a Hindu temple.

There are three basic elements to Hindu temple worship. First the **Havan**, which is an offering of fire and prayers to the gods. **Ghee**, or liquid butter, is placed on pieces of wood on a portable fire, while passages from the Vedas are recited. Then follows **Arti**, or the worship of light. A tray with five lights is moved from one side of the shrine to the other and then passed to the congregation who hold their hands over the flames and then on their foreheads. They may sing **bhajans**, or hymns, accompanied by a variety of musical instruments. Dance is important to Hinduism, especially since many hand movements have a special significance.

Hindu festivals and pilgrimages

Hindus love festivals and any opportunity to celebrate. The two most important Hindu festivals are **Holi** and **Diwali**. Holi is a Spring festival and takes place in February or March. It is a time for the telling of stories about the god Krishna and for playing practical jokes on one another, just as Krishna used to play jokes on the milkmaids. For this reason it is very much an outdoor festivity. Diwali means 'cluster of lights' and this festival takes place in October or November. At this time Hindus celebrate their New Year and they remember the occasion when **Lakshmi**, the goddess of prosperity, goodness and light, and wife of the god **Vishnu**, overthrew evil or darkness. People let off fireworks to ward off evil spirits, and effigies of **Ravana**, the demon king, may be burnt on a bonfire. It is also the time for all members of the family to renew their vows to one another.

Many Hindus go on pilgrimages to acquire merit and so improve their chances of getting a good rebirth. For them it is an act of devotion to the gods. **Benares** is the most important of the holy places and is situated on the river **Ganges**, itself a holy river. It is considered a great privilege to have one's ashes thrown into the Ganges. Often bottles of water from the Ganges are taken back to those unable to go on the pilgrimage. The gods Shiva and Rama in particular are associated with the city of Benares. Pilgrims also visit **Hardwar** and here, too, human ashes may be thrown into the river. **Vrindaban**, known as the birthplace of the god Krishna, is another holy place that many pilgrims regularly visit.

In India there are numerous holy places besides those mentioned and many Hindus travel extensively through India making a tour of the holy sites. For example; it is not unusual for a pilgrim to travel up the length of the River Ganges and then back down the opposite side; a tremendously long journey which indicates the degree of reverence attached to the holy river.

Chapter 12
Buddhism

Siddhartha Gautama

Siddhartha Gautama, or Gotama, was born in North India, at Kapilavastu, around 563 BC. He was a Hindu and member of the warrior caste, the son of a wealthy local lord. Though he had every need satisfied, he led a secluded life, as his father sheltered him from the rigours and realities of the outside world. It was not until he was twenty-nine, and happily married with one son, that he ventured out with his charioteer and saw for himself the extent of the suffering that existed in the world. He met an old man, a sick man, then a dead man and a monk, and was greatly moved by such an experience. He decided to leave his family and his life of ease and comfort and one night, secretly, he left for the forest. Having shaved his head and wearing old ragged clothes, he set out to seek the answer to suffering. He joined a band of ascetic Brahmins and, according to tradition, ate only a grain of rice a day for six years. He then became disillusioned with this style of life, realizing that it did not bring him any closer to discovering the reason for suffering.

One day he arrived at Gaya and sat under a tree, now called the **Bo tree,** or 'tree of enlightenment', since it was here that enlightenment, or true wisdom, came to him. He realised that the way to avoid suffering was to follow the **'Middle Way'** between extremes. After his enlightenment under the Bo tree he was called the **'Buddha',** or 'enlightened one'.

He preached his first sermon in a deer park near Benares and addressed, among others, the five monks who had travelled with him before his enlightenment. He then spent many years preaching to the people of India and explaining how they might gain release from the constant round of rebirths. After eating some poisoned food he died and was cremated at the age of eighty at Kusinara in 483 BC.

Buddhist writings

It should be pointed out at this stage that there are two types of Buddhism and these are practised in different parts of the world. Which Buddhist writings a follower accepts depends on the branch of Buddhism to which he belongs. Southern Buddhism, known as **'Theravada'** Buddhism, or 'the doctrine of the elders', is practised in Sri Lanka, Burma, Laos and Cambodia. It is also sometimes called **'Hinayana'** Buddhism, or the 'small vehicle'. Northern Buddhism, or **'Mahayana'** Buddhism, or the 'great vehicle', is practised in Tibet, China, Korea, Japan and Vietnam.

The canon of the Southern Buddhists is called the **Tipitaka**, or 'The Three Baskets' and it is written in the Pali language. Its Sanskrit name is 'Tripitaka'. It consists of rules for the monks and nuns, teachings of the Buddha, and further elaborations of the Buddha's teachings. The Northern Buddhists use the Pali Canon together with their writings and these constitute their own canon of scripture.

Buddhist beliefs and teachings

The Buddha believed that all life was impermanent and transitory and that there was no permanent soul. Man, he said, consists of a bundle of impermanent, changing states of being. These are called **'skandhas'**. The world is an illusion and one can free oneself from it and reach **'Nirvana'**, a state of perfect peace, or the extinguishing of all desire. This amounts to release from the constant wheel of existence. But it is something which each person must achieve on his own. There is no saviour in Buddhism to help him: each must work out his own salvation.

The Buddha taught that there were four **'Noble Truths'**:

1. All life is suffering.
2. Suffering is caused by desire.
3. Suffering can be cured by stopping desire.
4. The way to do this is to follow the **Eightfold Path**, that is, the middle way between asceticism and self-indulgence. It was thus possible, he said, for all men and women to achieve release from rebirth and hence from suffering.

The Eightfold Path states that the Buddhist should have:

1. the right view or understanding;
2. the right resolve and therefore the desire to leave aside worldly things;
3. the right way of speaking and control over his tongue;
4. the right conduct and behaviour;
5. the right means of earning a living. (This would involve, apart from other things, an occupation that was not concerned with killing animals.)
6. the right effort, so as to do what is good;
7. the right concentration and control of the mind;
8. the right form of meditation.

Initiation into Buddhism

One becomes a Buddhist by agreeing to follow the Buddhist way of life. The candidate makes an act of homage, such as the following: 'Adoration to Him, the Blessed One, the Worthy One, the Fully Enlightened One', and agrees to adopt the 'Three Refuges', which could be regarded as an act of faith:

I take refuge in the Buddha;
I take refuge in the Dhamma [the teaching of the Buddha];
I take refuge in the Sangha [the community of monks].

The layman must agree to abide by the following five precepts:

1. He must not kill an animal or human. This precept is clearly linked to the fifth of the eightfold path directives.
2. He must not steal.
3. He must not commit adultery.
4. He must not tell lies.
5. He must not drink alcohol.

There are a further five precepts which apply to the monk or **bhikkhu**:

6. He must not eat after noon.
7. He must not sing, dance or play music.
8. He must not sit on comfortable chairs.
9. He must not handle money.
10. He must not wear expensive clothes.

161

A Buddhist wishing to become a monk must also agree to give up all his possessions, owning only a begging bowl, a razor and a strainer, the last named to ensure that he does not accidentally kill an insect when he is eating. He must shave his head, wear a saffron robe and beg for his food in the neighbourhood. He will eat this at the time of his one meal, that is before noon. It is not uncommon for Theravada Buddhist boys to become monks for several months when they are quite young. They shave their heads, wear the saffron robes and submit themselves to the same rules as the monks.

Buddhist worship and festivals

Worship is of an individual nature in Buddhism. There is no set, formal worship. A Buddhist may worship in his home where a room may be set aside as a shrine, or he may worship in a temple. Both in the home and in the temple there will be a statue of the Buddha before whom the Buddhist will bow as a sign of reverence and then sit cross-legged on the floor. With his hands on his lap and his eyes closed he will begin meditation.

The major Buddhist festival is **Wesak** and on this day Buddhists remember the Buddha's birth, his enlightenment and his reaching Nirvana. It takes place in May and is a time for colourful processions through the streets. **Magha Puja** is the anniversary of the day when the Buddha gave his followers rules for them to follow. There are many other Buddhist festivals celebrated in different parts of the world. Various countries have a national festival to celebrate the coming of Buddhism to their land.

Chapter 13
Sikhism

Sikhism is one of the newest world religions and was founded by **Nanak,** a Hindu, who lived from AD 1469 to 1539, and came from Talwandi, a few miles from Lahore, in the Punjab and now in Pakistan. Nanak was familiar with the beliefs and customs of the Muslims as well as those of his own religion, and became dissatisfied and disillusioned with both. They seemed to Nanak to emphasize the wrong aspects of religion and to attach too much importance to outward show. He was concerned with what a man thought in his heart.

Nanak was convinced that there was only one God. When he was thirty he had a vision in which he was taken to God's court. After this, he considered that his mission in life was to preach to the people about belief in the one God. It was not important, he said, whether people were Muslims or Hindus, nor did it matter to what caste they belonged. He spent twenty years preaching to the people of India about his ideas regarding God, first on a series of missionary tours and then at Kartarpur.

Nanak was the first of the ten **Gurus**, a word meaning teacher and much venerated in Sikhism. Before he died Nanak appointed Lehna, whose name he changed to Angad, to succeed him as leader of the Sikh community and as God's messenger. The ten Gurus in Sikhism were:

1. Guru Nanak (1469–1539)
2. Guru Angad (1539–1552)
3. Guru Amar Das (1552–1574)
4. Guru Ram Das (1574–1581)
5. Guru Arjan (1581–1606)
6. Guru Hargobind (1606–1644)
7. Guru Har Rai (1644–1661)
8. Guru Har Krishan (1661–1664)
9. Guru Tegh Bahadur (1664–1675)
10. Guru Gobind Singh (1675–1708)

Sikh writings: the Guru Granth and the Dasam Granth

There are two principal writings in the Sikh religion. The first, formerly known as the **Adi Granth**, or First Collection, consists of writings by Guru Nanak, and also selections from the writings of Hindus and Muslims. These are hymns and poems in praise of God and are written in Punjabi. Since the time of Guru Gobind Singh, the Granth has been called the **Guru Granth Sahib**, as Gobind Singh said that, from that point on, the people should regard the Granth as their Guru or teacher. The **Dasam Granth** consists of the writings of Guru Gobind Singh which were collected together after his death.

Sikh beliefs and teachings

Sikhism prides itself on its simplicity and there are therefore few doctrinal ideas in the religion. As already indicated, Sikhs believe that there is only one God. They believe that he can be worshipped by all men and women of whatever caste. All are equal in the eyes of God. God is the creator of all living things and he loves and cares for them. This is illustrated by the following passage from the 'Japji', a long hymn at the beginning of the Granth:

> God is One,
> He is the True Name,
> The Maker and All-pervading Spirit
> Fearing nothing, hating no-one,
> A Being beyond time,
> Self-existent beyond birth,
> Revealed by the grace of the Guru.

According to Sikh thought it is impossible to describe God, yet he allows himself to be known. He is present in every human heart and in each life. Sikhs believe in reincarnation or rebirth, as in Hinduism, but they believe that **'moksha'**, that is salvation or release from life, is obtained through God's grace. It is a free gift from God.

Initiation ceremonies: the Khalsa and the five 'K's

The word **'Khalsa'** means 'pure' or 'dedicated ones', and is used to refer to the Sikh brotherhood. It was introduced by Guru Gobind Singh, the last of the Gurus, in 1699.

At their initiation all Sikhs have to adopt what are called the five 'K's. These are:

1. **Kesh**, that is uncut hair. This demonstrates their love for God.
2. The **Kangha**, a comb to keep their hair tidy.
3. The **Kirpan**, which is a short ceremonial two-edged sword representing their fight against evil.
4. **Kachs**, or short underpants. This is to remind them of the time in the past when they had to move quickly when under attack.
5. The **Kara**, or steel bracelet which is worn on the right wrist. This reminds them of the presence of God. In addition to these five things, all Sikhs wear a turban to keep their hair tidy. This forms part of their distinctive dress.

The candidate for admission into the Sikh community listens to an address on the Sikh faith given by one of the elder Sikhs. He, or she, is then given five handfuls of **'amrita'**, or nectar, to drink. This consists of sugar and water which has been mixed together in an iron bowl with the kirpan or sword. It is also placed on the initiate's eyes and hair. All men are given the name **'Singh'**, meaning 'lion', and all women are called **'Kaur'** or 'princess'.

Place of worship: the Gurdwara

There is no set day for worship in the Sikh religion and no set time to begin but custom has established a Sunday, at least in the West, as a convenient day for Sikhs to meet together. They meet at a **Gurdwara**, or Sikh temple, The word 'Gurdwara' means 'the door of the home of the Guru', and is so called because the Guru Granth, which is regarded as the living Guru, is housed there.

When Sikhs enter a Gurdwara they must remove their shoes and cover their heads, They bow before the Granth which can be seen on a cushion on a raised platform and under a canopy. They may place some food or money in a basket in front of the Granth. There are no seats in a Gurdwara and men and women sit cross-legged on the floor, generally men on the left and women on the right. They face in the direction of the Granth.

Though there is no formal pattern of worship, the following example of worship in a Gurdwara is fairly usual. A popular beginning is the singing of hymns in praise of God, and this might be accompanied on a variety of musical instruments. From this we see that in Sikhism worship is congregational in style. There may then be readings from the Granth, read by the Granthi, or reader, followed by a sermon. Special prayers, called **Ardas** are then recited, and the people share the **Karah Parshad**, which consists of milk, semolina, butter and sugar. This is passed round to all those present and a little is given to each. It is intended to demonstrate the equality of all men and women. After worshipping together everyone passes into the Gurdwara kitchen, called the **Langar**, where they have a communal meal together. Besides worship, a local Gurdwara may be a meeting place in the week for members of the local Sikh community, and it may also be used as a religious school where Sikh children are taught the scriptures.

Festivals and pilgrimages

The festival of Baisakhi takes place in April and is the beginning of the Sikh year. It was on this day in 1699 that Guru Gobind Singh initiated the Khalsa. It could be regarded as the birthday of Sikhism and for this reason new members of the faith are brought forward on this day. **Diwali**, also called the festival of Lights, is a famous Sikh festival, when Sikhs celebrate the victory of good over evil. It is celebrated in November. **Gurpurbs** are holidays associated with a Guru. In India on these days the Granth is carried round the streets in procession.

The Golden Temple at Amritsar, known as **Hari Mandir**, was built by the fifth Guru, Arjan and is situated in an artificial lake. Inside one can hear the Granth being recited continually by a band of readers. It is a natural place of pilgrimage for all Sikhs.

Further Reading

Chapters 1–3
Rattey, B.K. *A Short History of the Hebrews*
(Oxford University Press)
Anderson, B.W. *The Living World of the Old Testament*
(Longman)

Chapter 4
Guy, H.A. *The Life of Christ*
(Macmillan)
Campbell, D.B.J. *The Synoptic Gospels*
(John Murray)
Barrell, E.V. & K.G. *St Luke's Gospel*
(John Murray)

Chapters 5–6
Guy, H.A. *The Acts of the Apostles*
(Macmillan)
Ridley Lewis, E. *The Acts of the Apostles and the Letters of St Paul*
(James Clarke & Co)
Drane, J. *Paul*
(Lion Publishing)

Chapter 7
Herod, F.G. *Who Cares?*
(Methuen Educational)
Field, D. *Christianity in the Modern World*
(Hulton Educational)

Chapters 8–13
Owen Cole, W. *Five Religions in the Twentieth Century*
(Hulton Educational)
Whiting, J.R.S. *Religions of Man*
(Stanley Thornes)
Collinson, C. and Miller, C. *Believers*
(Edward Arnold)
Roadley, K.P. *Your Way and Mine*
(Edward Arnold)

Examination Hints

This section of the book provides candidates preparing for O Level and the CSE with some guidelines to bear in mind before the date of their examination. It is vital to prepare adequately and correctly for any examination. The right kind of planning is essential. Every year candidates fail in Religious Studies, as well as in other subjects, because they have not prepared in the right manner for the examination. They find themselves looking at the piece of paper on the desk with hardly an ordered thought in their heads. To be able to marshal your thoughts together on the day demands practice. It is folly to try and depend on good luck to save you. Every candidate must know the subject concerned thoroughly.

Preparatory details

So what must you do to assist your preparation for the examination? First of all, it is important to ensure that you have a copy of the latest regulations and syllabus of the Examining Board that is setting your examination. Examining Boards vary a great deal in their requirements and their expectations of candidates. If you are a private candidate it is important to bear in mind that some Examining Boards may specify which examination a private candidate may take and which he may not take. It would be very foolish indeed to prepare for an examination for two years only to find that you cannot sit the examination with the Board of your choice. Remember also that the regulations of Examining Boards may change from year to year. If you are a pupil preparing for the subject as an internal candidate at a secondary school, then your Head of Department and the member of staff responsible for examinations will attend to such matters.

Seek out **past papers** on the subject and study them carefully to see what questions you could tackle without too much difficulty. Try to find common areas of interest in questions of different papers. You can always write to the Examining Board and ask them for past papers in your subject. They will gladly provide you with details of the fee that they have to charge for publishing the papers—this is generally small.

There should be some provision for you to sit a 'mock' or 'trial' examination in your subject. This is useful in so far as it helps to prepare you for the conditions of the examination. It will also provide you with some valuable practice in timing your answers. You will then feel less nervous or apprehensive on the day but remember that everyone will be 'in the same boat' as you. Most people are at least a little nervous of examinations and some even view the event with trepidation. There is no need for you to feel this way if you prepare adequately and comprehensively.

Organizing yourself before the examination

You must study your set books and know them well. That may seem obvious to you but this point cannot be overemphasized. Clearly, you must **know the subject on which you are being examined from every angle**. First, read the book through from beginning to end to refresh your memory of the general themes. Then read the book in sections, referring to the notes that you have compiled over the total period of preparation for the examination. You should recall the discussions that you had with your teacher and fellow pupils and then study the commentary in the set text.

As far as Bible study is concerned, you will need to ensure that you have a correct note of the passages for study. You may be required to study the whole of the book of Amos, for example, or just some chapters and verses of that book.

Make sure you have the right version of the Bible—otherwise, you may not easily recognize a passage in a context question and you will not have the time to stop and ponder a long time over it.

Do not rely for your answers on devotional comments and explanations of the text. Remember that in any examination you must demonstrate your objective knowledge of the subject and your approach must therefore be objective on all occasions.

When revising for the examination you should compile your

revision notes in as orderly a manner as possible. Have **some form of system**, even if it is clear only to yourself, so that you **know where to find material relating to a certain aspect of the subject at a moment's notice**. If you are preparing for the part of the paper dealing with the New Testament, for example, collect together a list of all the occasions when Jesus taught in parables, all the references to prayer, all the instances of conflict between Jesus and the authorities, all the references to the Kingdom of God. Have in this respect a **thematic approach. Collect together all the references to similar themes**. While you must endeavour to know your subject well, however, it is natural that some sections or themes of the subject should interest you more than others and these you should learn in particular. There is no harm in having certain 'pet' parts of the syllabus that you know well.

Sitting the examination

It is sensible to arrive early for the examination so that you can find the room and settle down to compose your thoughts. The invigilator (the person who supervises the examination) will ask you to write down your name and examination number on your paper, so remember to take the number to the Examination Centre, along with any other materials that you may need, such as spare pens, pencils, rubbers and rulers. You will probably have to write down the Centre number as well.

Check how many questions you have to answer. The questions may also be in parts. **Be sure of the alternatives possible**. There may be different parts of the paper which are assessed separately or in a different manner. You may have to answer three questions from Section 1 and four questions from Section 2. **Do not answer more questions than the number required. You will not gain extra marks for this**. Indeed, you will be wasting time in doing so since this time should be spent on answering other questions. **Spend at least five minutes reading through the question paper** before deciding which questions to answer. Your first impression of the paper may be quite wrong. Be sure you understand the meaning of the questions you will tackle and then **spend a few minutes planning each answer**. Don't forget to **allow an equal amount of time for each question. Check on the total amount of time allowed for the paper!**

It should go without saying that your **writing should be legible**. Attempt in all circumstances to **ensure that your spelling is accurate**. In this way you will render the Examiner's job that much easier. Unconsciously, if not consciously, he may in this way be more favourably inclined towards you! You will also be moving in the right direction if you **answer the question in the manner the Examining Board suggests**. A lot of care and attention have been given to the exact framing of the question long before it reaches your desk. Do not assume that the examination is simply an opportunity to tell the Examiner everything you know about the subject. **He is looking for specific facts in every question. Make sure you give these facts**.

Some Examining Boards, particularly CSE Boards, give an indication in the margin of the question paper of how the questions are marked. They will tell you the maximum number of marks that you may gain for each part of the question. **Study this carefully so that you devote more time to a part of the question where you could gain twelve marks than one where you would gain six marks.**

Be prepared for a **compulsory context question**. There is usually a choice within this question, however. To comment on the passages set in the context question you will need to know the set books thoroughly. Here again, though, it is **not an opportunity to write everything you know about the passage**. There are often very **specific questions** attached to the passages and you must answer these fully.

Be as **clear** as you can in the **meaning** of what you write. Do not give the Examiner the impression that you are muddled in your approach. Furthermore, do not leave everything to the Examiner's imagination. He does not know what is in your mind and he cannot read your thoughts. Remember that he is looking for factual material and relevant argument. Show that you understand the significance of the topics you have chosen.

Finally, leave a few minutes at the end of the examination to read through your work. This is important because the omission of one or two words in a particular sentence could render the sense of a whole section incomprehensible to the Examiner. It is possible that one word left out could leave the Examiner with the opposite impression from that which you wish to convey.

Key Facts Revision Section

Old Testament History
to the Division of the Kingdom

The Jews are regarded as God's chosen people.
–Early myths about the world and the creation of mankind, as depicted in the book of Genesis
–Noah as 'the one blameless man of his time'
–The first covenant between God and man is initiated.

Abraham and the beginning of Hebrew religion, c 1700 BC
–The Hebrews settle in Canaan.
–Abraham's agreement with God–God promises Abraham that he will inherit the land–Circumcision is seen as part of the agreement with God.
–God tests Abraham's faith and obedience using his son Isaac. Abraham begins to understand what God expects from him.
–Isaac marries Rebecca.

Esau and Jacob
–Jacob tricks his brother Esau out of his birthright.
–Jacob's dream and the renewal of the covenant with God
–Jacob's twelve sons

Joseph, the favourite son of Jacob, and his jealous brothers
–Brothers put Joseph in a pit and then sell him to the Ishmaelites.
–As a slave in Egypt he interprets Pharaoh's dream.
–Joseph rises to a powerful position in Egypt during the years of famine.
–Joseph and his brothers are reconciled.

The birth of Moses during the reign of Rameses II
–Moses kills an Egyptian taskmaster.
–His call by God, known as Yahweh, at Mount Horeb
–Moses' dealings with Pharaoh: he requests Pharaoh to free the people from slavery and let them go. Pharaoh refuses and the country is beset with plagues. The Israelites are not affected–The origin of the Passover festival

The escape from Egypt
– The Hebrews encounter problems in the wilderness.
– Moses becomes their law-giver – He delivers the Ten Commandments to them from God – The Covenant with God is renewed.
– The worship of God is elaborated with the 'Shema' and the making of the Ark of the Covenant.

Joshua succeeds Moses as leader of the people.
– They conquer Canaan in stages.
– A new Covenant is made with God.
– Jericho and Ai are captured.
– A confederacy of tribes is formed.

The Judges arise as local heroes. The most important are Othniel, Ehud, Deborah, Gideon, Jephthah, and Samson. All see themselves as fighting on God's behalf.

The call and work of Samuel
– He serves under Eli, a priest.
– He becomes a Nazarite and a Judge of the people.
– Hophni and Phinehas, the sons of Eli, are killed fighting the Philistines.
– The Ark is captured by the Philistines.
– The people ask Samuel for a king.

The beginning of the monarchy
– **Saul**, a Benjamite, is anointed by Samuel and declared king.
– After a series of battles Saul is rejected by God – David calms Saul during fits of depression.
– David forms a friendship with Jonathan, Saul's son.
– David laments the death of Saul and Jonathan on Mount Gilboa.

David's reign
– David captures Jerusalem and makes his capital there – the building of his palace.
– David is condemned by Nathan for killing Uriah and marrying his wife, Bathsheba.
– The renewal of the Covenant
– The possibility of David as the author of some of the Psalms

−David unites the tribes and the kingdom.

Solomon's reign
−Solomon requests wisdom from God.
−The possibility of Solomon as the author of some of the Proverbs
−Solomon builds a Temple for the worship of God.
−He taxes the people and uses forced labour.
−He shows tolerance towards the introduction of other religions

The division of the kingdom on Solomon's death between Rehoboam in Judah and Jeroboam in Israel.

The Old Testament Prophets

The work of the prophets−Ecstatic and writing prophets
−Elijah and Elisha condemn injustices.
−Elijah encounters the prophets of Baal.
−Elijah denounces the unfaithfulness of the people.
−Jezebel, Ahab's wife aims to abolish Israelite worship.
−Elijah challenges the prophets of Baal on Mount Carmel.
−The people are urged to reject useless gods.
−Elijah attacks the king over the incident of Naboth and his vineyard.
−Elijah ascends into heaven.

Elijah is succeeded by Elisha
−Legendary stories are associated with him.
−Naaman, the Syrian leper, is healed.
−The prophetic revolution: Jehu is commissioned to purge the country of Baal worship.

Amos becomes the first of the writing prophets and first of the twelve 'minor' prophets.

175

–He presents the people with messages of doom.
–Amos tells the people that Yahweh is God of all nations who demands justice for the poor–He emphasizes to the people the difference between right and wrong.
–The people will be judged.

Hosea, the prophet of loving kindness presents his message to the people.
–The people had broken the covenant with God.
–God would forgive the people, if they repented, as Hosea forgave Gomer, his prostitute wife.

Isaiah One of Jerusalem
–Isaiah sees God as the Holy One of Israel.
–He speaks of oppression in the country and the judgment to come on the people.
–The people are to trust in God.
–Isaiah speaks of a sign, that of a child, a messiah.

Micah speaks of the wickedness of the people–even the priests are following wicked ways.

The achievements of Josiah
–The Book of the Law is discovered in the Temple in 621 BC.
–Josiah renews the covenant with God.
–Josiah makes a number of religious reforms.

The role of Jeremiah as a spiritual teacher
–He urges the people to repent and refers to the judgment to come.
–He tells the people that God demands a personal response from them–God wants a new relationship with them–The Law should be written on their hearts.
–The people are urged not to join in political alliances.
–Nebuchadnezzar of Babylon attacks Jerusalem.
–There are three deportations to Babylon.
–Jeremiah recommends the people settle down to a new life in Babylon.
–Jeremiah is taken to Egypt.
–The province is merged with the northern territory.

The Jewish Exile and Return

The condition of the exiles in Babylon
–They are allowed freedom and permitted to practise their faith.
–They hope for an early return.
–The prophet **Ezekiel** tells the people that everyone is responsible for his own actions–God is depicted as the Shepherd of the people.
–House meetings replace worship in the Temple.
–The scriptures are written down.
–Study of the Jewish Law develops. Rules are set out relating to the form worship should take.
–The importance of circumcision is emphasized.

Isaiah Two or Deutero-Isaiah (chapters 40–55), or the **Isaiah of Babylon**, describes God as all-powerful.
–Deutero-Isaiah teaches about the 'Suffering Servant'.
–Cyrus the Persian is seen by Isaiah as the deliverer of the Jewish people–Cyrus issues a decree permitting Jews to return to Judea.
–Many Jews return to rebuild the city walls and meet opposition from the Samaritans.

The rebuilding of the Temple
–The prophets Haggai and Zechariah encourage the people in their efforts to rebuild the Temple.

Isaiah Three (chapters 56–66)
–Isaiah gives a gloomy picture of the situation in Judea after the return from Babylon.

Nehemiah and Ezra and their return to Jerusalem, Nehemiah in 444 BC and Ezra in 397 BC.
–Nehemiah encourages the people in their work on the city walls.
–He also encourages strict observance of the Jewish Law.
–Mixed marriages are banned.
–Ezra arrives and reads the Law to the people and takes Nehemiah's reforms further.
–Jews were to be divorced from their foreign wives.

The end of the Persian Empire comes with its defeat by Alexander the Great of Macedon—The Greek period of Jewish history begins.
−The Ptolemies and the Seleucids reign over the people and both in turn encourage Greek thought and culture.
−The rule of the high-priests begins in Palestine.
−The Septuagint, or LXX, or Greek version of the Jewish scriptures is written at Alexandria in Egypt.
−Antiochus IV, Epiphanes, bans Jewish worship in 168 BC.
−There is much religious harassment of the Jews.
−The revolt of the Maccabees.
−The role of Mattathias and his sons, Judas, John, Simon, Jonathan and Eleazar.
−The Hasmonean dynasty of high-priest kings begins.

The Life and Teaching of Jesus Christ

Characteristics of the Synoptic Gospels: Matthew, Mark and Luke
−John's Gospel is seen to be distinct from the others.
−Mark as the first Gospel
−Matthew and Luke as dependent on Mark
−Another source called 'Q'
−Luke wrote for Gentile Christians and Matthew wrote his Gospel for Jewish Christians.

The political background to the life of Jesus
Jesus is born a Jew in Palestine, which is part of the Roman Empire.

The announcement of the conception of John the Baptist and of Jesus
−Zechariah is to call his son John.
−The announcement of the conception of Jesus to Mary by Gabriel
−Mary's song: The Magnificat

The birth of John the Baptist and of Jesus
–Zechariah's song of praise: the Benedictus
–John is seen as the forerunner of Jesus.
–Jesus is born during the reign of the emperor Augustus.
–He is visited by shepherds and 'magi'.
–Jesus is presented in the Temple for circumcision.
–The greeting by Simeon and Anna
–Jesus and his parents visit the Temple when he is twelve. He is missing from the family group and is found back in the Temple.

John the Baptist's message
–The people are told to repent.
–Jesus is baptized by John and is then tempted in the wilderness.

Jesus' early work in Galilee
–Jesus fails to win over the people of Nazareth.
–He preaches in Capernaum.
–He appoints twelve assistants: Peter, James, John, Andrew, Philip, Bartholomew, Matthew, Thomas, John the son of Alphaeus, Simon called the Zealot, Judas the son of James, and Judas Iscariot.

Jesus comes into conflict with the Jewish authorities.
1. He heals a paralytic.
2. He calls Levi, a tax collector, to become one of his followers.
3. He answers a question about fasting.
4. An incident in the cornfields: Jesus is accused of working on the Sabbath.
5. He heals a man with a withered hand.

Jesus' miracles
1. Jesus heals the centurian's servant at Capernaum.
2. Jesus heals the widow's son at Nain.
3. Jesus stills the storm on the lake.
4. Jesus rids a man of demons: the Gadarene madman.
5. Jesus heals Jairus' daughter.
6. Jesus feeds the five thousand.

–John the Baptist asks for a sign.

–Jesus has strained relationships with the Pharisees and Sadducees.

–The **Pharisees** believe in the written Law and the Oral Law. They also believe in a resurrection, Hades, a final judgment and the coming messiah.

–The **Sadducees**, the lay aristocracy, are leaders of the Sanhedrin. They observe only the written Law and do not subscribe to a belief in a resurrection and additions to the Law.

–The **Zealots** are fierce revolutionaries whereas the **Essenes** seek to achieve the rule of God on earth by means of prayer and meditation.

–Jesus' teaching is presented by the Gospel writers Matthew and Luke in the form of a **sermon**.

–Matthew has the **Sermon on the Mount** and Luke has the **Sermon on the Plain**.

–The Beatitudes and Woes: the true follower of Jesus is described as one concerned about spiritual matters.

–Jesus presents his listeners with the 'Golden Rule'.

Jesus teaches by means of parables and tells his disciples about the **Kingdom of God**:
1. The sower
2. The lamp
3. The seed growing secretly
4. The mustard seed
5. The leaven
6. The treasure and pearl merchant
7. The net full of fishes

–**Parables of the lost**
1. The lost sheep
2. The lost coin
3. The lost son

Peter's confession of faith at Caesarea Philippi: he proclaims Jesus as the messiah.

–Jesus is on a mountain with Peter, James and John, and is **transfigured** before them–They hear the words of God.

The journey to Jerusalem
–Jesus heals ten lepers.
–James and John request places of honour beside Jesus.
–Jesus warns the disciples of the cost of being a disciple.

Jesus in Jerusalem
–Jesus enters Jerusalem on Palm Sunday, riding on a colt–He is greeted by people waving palms.
–Jesus drives out the traders and money changers from the Temple.
–He teaches in the Temple on several days–Discussions with the Pharisees and Sadducees–Jesus is questioned about his authority for his teaching and about the payment of taxes–The Sadducees question him about the resurrection.
–Judas offers to betray Jesus.

The Last Supper (held at the time of the Passover)
–Jesus distributes bread and wine signifying the new covenant.
–Peter is told that he would deny Jesus three times.

The trials of Jesus
–The trials are considered as interrogations rather than trials.
–Jesus is accused of blasphemy and treason.
–The responsibility of Pilate
–Barabbas is freed.

The crucifixion and death of Jesus
–Jesus is flogged and taken to a place called the Skull, (Golgotha), and is placed on a cross.
–Jesus' words from the cross and his death
–Joseph of Arimathea requests from Pilate the body of Jesus.

The Resurrection appearances
1. The discovery of the empty tomb
2. Jesus appears to two of the disciples on the road to Emmaus.
3. Jesus appears before the disciples at Jerusalem on the evening of Easter Day.
4. Jesus appears to the disciples in Galilee.
–Jesus' ascension at Bethany.

The Acts of the Apostles

–The development of Christianity in the first century:
–The Acts of the Apostles–Luke as the author
–The disciples wait for the coming of the Holy Spirit.
–Peter assumes the leadership of the community of believers.
–Matthias is chosen to replace Judas Iscariot.
–The Day of Pentecost: the Holy Spirit descends upon the disciples.
–Baptism is adopted as the Christian initiation ceremony.

–The preaching and healing ministry of **Peter**–He works with John.
–They are arrested and appear before the Sanhedrin–Gamaliel assumes a significant role.

–The early organization of the Church–**Barnabas** shows his generosity, in contrast to Ananias and Sapphira who attempted to deceive the apostles and God.
–The seven deacons are appointed to care for the Hellenistic widows: Stephen, Philip, Prochorus, Nicanor, Timon, Parmenas and Nicolas of Antioch.
–**Stephen** becomes the **first Christian martyr**–His death by stoning is witnessed by Saul of Tarsus.

–Philip preaches and performs miracles in Samaria–he meets Simon Magus, a magician.
–Philip meets the Ethiopian eunuch an official of the Queen of Ethiopia and baptizes him.

Saul is converted while on the way to Damascus with the intention of persecuting the Christians. Ananias, a Christian disciple lays his hands on Saul and he is baptized.

–Peter is recognized as leader of the early Christian community and goes on a preaching tour. At Caesarea he converts Cornelius, a Roman centurian and therefore a Gentile.
–Barnabas works with Saul–Saul is now called Paul.

–**Paul's first missionary journey** with Barnabas, and John Mark
–Paul's tour of preaching and healing lasts two years.
–He visits: Antioch in Syria, Seleucia, Salamis, Paphos, Perga in Pamphylia, Antioch in Pisidia, Iconium, Lystra, Derbe, Lystra, Iconium and Antioch.

–The question of how to treat Jewish Christians and Gentile converts is resolved at the **Council of Jerusalem**. Gentile Christians are excused from the Jewish rite of circumcision.

Paul's second missionary journey with Silas–The possibility that Luke travelled with them
–From Antioch they went to: Derbe and Lystra, Troas, Samothrace, Neapolis, Philippi, Amphipolis, Apollonia, Thessalonica, Berea, Athens, Corinth, Cenchrea, Ephesus, Caesarea, and then Jerusalem.

–Paul makes a **third missionary journey** and from Antioch visits Galatia, and Phrygia, Ephesus, Macedonia, Greece, Philippi, Troas, Assos, Mitylene, Chios, Samos, Miletus, Cos, Rhodes, Patara, Tyre, Ptolemais, Caesarea and Jerusalem.

Paul at Jerusalem
–Paul undergoes a Nazarite vow–He is accused by Asian Jews of teaching against the Jewish religion.
–He is taken to the Roman barracks and proclaims his Roman citizenship.
–He is taken to Caesarea.
–Paul appears before the Roman Governor Felix and then before Festus–He also appears before King Agrippa II.
–Paul is taken to Rome by ship.
–They are shipwrecked on Malta.
–Paul arrives at Rome–He remains there for two years.
–He is then freed or executed.

The Letters of Paul

–The letters of Paul reflect the atmosphere of the early Christian communities.

1 and 2 Thessalonians: These letters were written from Corinth on Paul's second missionary journey.

–Certain accusations had been made against Paul.

–There were problems regarding the second coming of Jesus.

–Paul tells his readers that all Christians will be raised up together at the resurrection; in the meantime, they are to **wait** patiently for the occasion and to work as usual–They have faced persecution well.

1 and 2 Corinthians: There were possibly four letters in the original Corinthian correspondence. 1 Corinthians was written from Ephesus on the third missionary journey.

–Paul had heard disturbing news from the people of Corinth. They were forming cliques, there was immorality among the community and they did not have the right attitude towards their worship and the prospect of the resurrection.

–Paul defends his authority and rebukes the people.

Galatians: This letter is concerned with Christian freedom and the relationship between Jewish and Gentile Christians.

–Paul says there is no need for Gentile Christians to be circumcised.

–The most important thing is faith–The Law is a temporary matter. They are to live like Christ.

Romans: This letter is a systematic account of Paul's thinking:

1. Man's relationship with God–Righteousness is to be obtained through faith–In this respect the Jews and Gentiles are alike.

2. The Jews have rejected the Messiah and so the Gospel is preached to the Gentiles.

3. Regarding Christian behaviour, Christians are to dedicate themselves to God.

4. The final section consists of personal greetings.

Colossians, Philemon, Ephesians, and Philippians are often called the Captivity Letters as they were probably written by Paul from prison.

Colossians: Referring to false teachers, who said that Christians should follow the Jewish Law and attain to a secret wisdom, Paul claims that true knowledge comes from God.

Philemon: This letter is about a runaway slave called Onesimus, whose master Philemon is urged to forgive him and accept him back.

Ephesians: This was possibly a circular letter sent to the churches of Asia. It is a thanksgiving for Christ and the Christian Church. Paul sets out the duties of Christians within the family.

Philippians: This letter consists of personal matters. Paul thanks the people for their support and warns them against disunity and Judaizers.

1 and 2 Timothy and Titus: These letters are usually known as the Pastoral Letters. They contain advice about the work and duties of a Christian pastor and also warnings about false teachings.

The Bible and current issues

Personal and family issues: love, sex and courtship
–The family was very important in Old Testament times.
–The need for sincerity in one's feelings
–Relationships involve commitment.
–Love forms the basis of all personal relationships.
–The New Testament is not a manual regarding personal conduct–It only gives general advice.
–In the teaching of Jesus marriage is an order of creation and in

the New Testament as a whole it is seen as a life-long commitment.
– The different interpretation by Paul is explained by the fact that he expected the early return of Jesus.
– Extra-marital relationships are not approved of.
– Divorce is not favoured.
– Right relationships are encouraged between members of the family.

The individual in society: work, the use of money and leisure
– In both the Old and New Testaments work is much favoured.
– Everything belongs to God, including wealth – People are stewards of what God has provided.
– The sabbath is an opportunity for rest.

Alcohol and drugs – Alcohol is accepted in the Old and New Testament but not drunken behaviour.
– There are no specific details regarding the use of drugs.

Problems of society: discrimination of class, colour and religion
– People are made in the likeness of God and so everyone is regarded as equal – This idea is expressed in the Old Testament – In the New Testament Jesus and Paul are opposed to discrimination.
– Tolerance and understanding are encouraged on the part of the believer.

Law and order – The Old Testament provides much information regarding the personal life of the Israelites.
– In the New Testament Jesus and Paul both emphasize that one should respect the State and all authority.

Wealth and poverty – There is nothing new in being poor, as the New Testament demonstrates.
– One should give to the poor.
– James in his letter points out that faith without action is lifeless.

Evil and suffering – In the Old Testament these are related but in the New Testament Jesus undertakes suffering on the part of others.

–The Christian bears his own cross–Following Christ will bring suffering.
–We find the idea that faith in Christ will overcome evil.

War and Peace The question of how to regard pacifism is raised and the 'just' war.

Judaism

–**Jewish Writings:** The Jewish Bible consists of twenty-four books. It has three parts: The Law, the Prophets, and the Writings. There is also a collection of writings called the Apocrypha and the Talmud.
–**Jewish beliefs and teachings** are summed up in the Ten Commandments and the Thirteen Principles of Maimonides.
–**Initiation ceremonies:** Circumcision and Bar Mitzvah: Circumcision takes place on the eighth day and Bar Mitzvah when a Jewish boy reaches the age of thirteen.
–**Jewish Worship** takes place in the Jewish home and in the synagogue.
–**Jewish fasts and festivals:** Rosh Hashanah, Yom Kippur, Succoth, Chanucah, Purim, Pesach and Shavuot
–**Special food customs:** Jews must not mix meat and dairy food, and they must not eat pork or birds of prey.

Christianity

–**Christian Scriptures:** The Old Testament is divided up into 39 books while there are 27 books in the New Testament. These form the canon (official list of books).

—**Christian beliefs and teachings** are summed up in the Creeds, such as the Apostles' Creed.

—**Initiation ceremonies:** Infant baptism is practised today but also believers' baptism. Confirmation takes place when a boy or girl reaches his/her teens.

—**Worship:** Christians worship in church on Sundays. Worship is congregational in nature with a priest or minister officiating. Important services are the Holy Communion, otherwise known as the Eucharist, and Mattins, or the Morning Service.

—**Fasts and festivals:** The Christian Year consists of: Advent, Christmas, Epiphany, Ash Wednesday, Lent, with Palm Sunday, Good Friday, Easter Day, Ascension Day, Whitsunday and Trinity.

—**Christian pilgrimages** to holy places: Some Christians visit holy places such as: Lourdes, Fatima, Knock, Glastonbury, Canterbury, Walsingham, Lindisfarne and Holy Island.

Islam

—**Muhammad the Prophet:** He was dissatisfied with the life and conditions of the people of Mecca and especially with the social conditions and the polytheism that was practised there. He began meditating and received visions from the angel Gabriel who told him to recite what he heard. He preached to the Meccans about Allah and when he was ridiculed left for Yathrib (Medina).

—**Islamic writings:** The Qur'an is the holy book of Islam and consists of the words of Allah for his people. The Hadith is a collection of the words of Muhammad,

—The **Five Pillars of Islam** are:

1. Shahada or Creed of Islam. There is no God but Allah and Muhammad is his messenger.
2. Salat or prayer
3. Saum or fasting
4. Zakat or gift offering
5. Hajj or pilgrimage

−**Fasts and festivals:** Muslims fast during the month of Ramadan which is followed by the festival of Id-al-Fitre. At the end of the pilgrimage to Mecca, Muslims celebrate the festival called Id-al-Adha.

Hinduism

−**Hindhu writings** are of two types: 'sruti' or 'revealed' writings, such as the Vedas and the Upanishads, and 'smrti' or 'remembered' writings, such as the Epics Mahabharata and the Ramayana, the Laws of Manu and the Puranas.
−**Beliefs and teachings:** there is a Universal Spirit called Brahman who is worshipped thrqugh the gods. The gods have earthly forms called avatars. Hindus believe in ahimsa or harmlessness. There are four stages to life and reincarnation in another life after this one. The caste system is important in Hinduism though there have been moves to dissolve it.
−**Initiation** to Hinduism for a Hindu child is by means of the sacred thread.
−Hindus worship in a puja room or in a temple. There is no set day for worship.
−**Hindu festivals: Holi**, the Spring festival and **Diwali**, the Autumn festival of light.
−**Pilgrimages** are made to such holy places as Benares, Hardwar and Vrindaban.

Buddhism

−Siddhartha Gautama was a Hindu who sought the meaning of suffering in life and became 'enlightened' under the Bo tree at Gaya. He was called the Buddha and preached the Middle Way.

—**Buddhist writings** consist of the Tipitaka or Three Baskets for Southern Buddhists (Theravada) and the Tipitaka with other writings for Northern Buddhists (Mahayana).

—**Buddhist beliefs and teachings:** All life is impermanent. One seeks Nirvana by following the Four Noble Truths and the Eightfold Path.

—**Initiation** into Buddhism is by adopting the Three Refuges and the Five Precepts.

—**Buddhist worship and festivals:** Worship in Buddhism is individual in nature and does not assume a formal approach. It can take place anywhere. The main celebrations in Buddhism are: the Buddha's birth, his enlightenment and his reaching Nirvana.

Sikhism

—**Nanak**, the founder, preached to the people about the one God. He said caste was not important. He was the first of the Gurus.

—**Sikh writings** consist of the Guru Granth Sahib and the Dasam Granth.

—**Sikh beliefs and teachings:** God can be worshipped by all people. It is not possible to describe him. Salvation is a free gift from him.

—**Initiation ceremony:** the Khalsa—all Sikhs must adopt the five 'K's—this was introduced by Guru Gobind Singh.

—**Place of worship:** the Gurdwara—Worship is congregational in nature and consists of readings from the Granth and singing hymns. There is no set day or time for worship. There is a meal in the langar after the service.

—**Festivals and pilgrimages:** Baisakhi takes place in Spring and on this occasion Sikhs remember how the Khalsa was introduced. Diwali is a festival of lights and on this occasion Sikhs celebrate the victory of good over evil. Sikhs make a pilgrimage if they can to the Hari Mandir Temple at Amritsar.

Index

192